George J. Whyte-Melville

The True Cross

A Legend of the Church

George J. Whyte-Melville

The True Cross
A Legend of the Church

ISBN/EAN: 9783337255824

Printed in Europe, USA, Canada, Australia, Japan

Cover: Foto ©Lupo / pixelio.de

More available books at **www.hansebooks.com**

THE TRUE CROSS.

A Legend of the Church.

BY

G. J. WHYTE-MELVILLE,

AUTHOR OF "BLACK BUT COMELY," "SARCHEDON," ETC.

New Edition.

LONDON:
WARD, LOCK, AND CO., WARWICK HOUSE,
SALISBURY SQUARE, E.C.

[*All Rights Reserved.*]

CONTENTS.

INTRODUCTION.

A VISION OF THE NIGHT.

		PAGE
BOOK I.—THE SEED	. . . .	1
,, II.—THE ARK	. . . . . .	4
,, III.—THE TREE	. . . .	10
,, IV.—THE BEAM	. . . . . .	13
,, V.—THE POOL	. . . .	19
,, VI.—THE CENTURION	. . . . . .	22

THE TRUE CROSS.

A Legend of the Church.

INTRODUCTION.

A VISION OF THE NIGHT.

I.

ONCE it befell that in a Great Lone Land
    I seemed to wander, sleeping while I lay,
    Nor hope I had at heart, nor help at hand,
Nor friend to guide and cheer me on the way,
Nor pilgrim's staff my faltering steps to stay:
But doubt and fear my spirit to consume,
    And round me gleams, too pale for light of day,
Reflected on the waste, and, in the gloom,
Faint, sickening airs, like those that hang about a tomb

II.

And through the dusk of wavering shadows, where
A dull earth melted in a duller sky,
The waft of beating wings, that longed to bear
Some vexed, unquiet spirit, fain to fly,
But downward urged by pressure from on high,
Yet thirsting for the fount where daylight streams,
While doomed in outer darkness here to lie.
Surely, a land of ghosts—a land of dreams—
Where every shifting shape is other than it seems!

III.

And high above me, threatening from afar,
Omen of dire confusion and affright,
Burned in the murky skies a blood-red star,
Fierce as a beacon, flashing through the night
To warn the nations with its baleful light,
That Death and Strife shall ride abroad ere noon;
Then, turning from its glow mine aching sight,
Behold!—twin herald of destruction—soon
Rose from the level earth a broad and blood-red Moon

INTRODUCTION.

IV.

Strange and fantastic objects thus I saw,
Called into being by the glare it shed—
Visions to bid my heart stand still with awe,
Dim, shadowy shapes and phantoms of the Dead.
While ever, like a funeral pall outspread,
Sad, slow, and solemn, moved from place to place
A sable cloud of mourning overhead,
And figures passed before me, with the trace
Of hopeless doom declared on every stricken face.

V.

Then, as the light grew stronger, I beheld
Each phase of mortal sorrow and despair.
One, by a life's affliction crushed and quelled,
Betrayed in livid lip and stony stare,
The pangs a broken heart had learned to bear,
Too sad to mourn, too humbled to revile;
Another did but traverse here and there,
With restless eyes aflame, and reckless smile,
Fierce as a wild beast trapped, but all untamed the while.

VI.

Some, as with burden of their sorrows bowed,
Crept through the shadows, crouching lowly down;
Some in defiance walked, erect and proud,
With haughty brows, that seemed in scorn to frown
Beneath the torture of an iron crown,
White-heated, till the brain was scorched and seared;
And some with stealthy gait, and girded gown,
Prowled in each other's footsteps, flouted, jeered,
Aimed unsubstantial blows, and glared, and disappeared.

VII.

But all were silent—silent as the leaf
That noiseless Autumn nips from off the tree—
Silent as sudden agony of grief,
That numbs us ere we struggle to be free,
And cry aloud to One we cannot see,
Imploring Him who made to spare and save—
Silent as Winter on an arctic sea,
Hushed to a frozen wind, a fettered wave:
As peaceful childhood's sleep—as troubled manhood's
grave.

VIII.

And through the tufted herbage, dank and cold,
In silence while I passed with silent tread,
A chill came curdling o'er me, for, behold,
My white and naked feet were dabbled red
With ghastly moisture by the grasses shed,
That looked and smelt like blood! And then I knew,
Surely as though 'twere whispered by the Dead,
How all the waste was crimson with the dew
Of all the murders done, the murderous ages through.

IX.

But, faint and feeble, still I stumbled on,
Nor dared to hope that I might reach the end
Ere courage wholly failed, and strength was gone,
Unless the hand of mercy should extend
Some pledge whereon my weakness might depend--
A sign, ere light had faded in despair,
My steps to guide, my wanderings to befriend.
While yet was scarce conceived the unspoken prayer,
Behold! a shadowy Cross loomed through the shadowy air.

X.

And every phantom, as it flitted past,
Bowed in acknowledged homage at the sight;
Its woeful burden earthward while it cast,
And hurried on, as though to claim of right
A shelter from the brooding storms of night!
Yet none that once had seen it turned again,
But seemed impelled, by some resistless might,
To find a certain solace for their pain,
And seek a soul's salvation, surely not in vain.

XI.

Here was a figure, stately in the pride
Of manhood's strength and stature, tall and brave,
But scowling, haggard-faced, and gloomy-eyed—
A rebel, who had thought it scorn to crave
Forgiveness on the threshold of the grave;
Yet now, before that holy sign, constrained
In meek submission suppliant hands to wave—
Hands that from deeds of blood had not refrained,
By no compunction stayed, by no regard restrained.

XII

And here a woman, with her hair unbound,
And brows of beauty, lustrous, though defiled
With shame that bade her grovel on the ground,
Clasped in her shapely arms a little child
With close embraces, and caresses wild—
And thus a mother's lesson fain to teach,
Uplifted to the Cross her babe, that smiled,
And stretched its tiny hands as though to reach
And hold the priceless Truth that creeds are framed to preach.

XIII.

Next came a troop of children, clad in white,
Fresh as a bank of flowers in early Spring,
With fair young faces, innocent and bright,
And voices sweet as woodland birds, to sing
A loving carol for their Lord and King;
Till by the angels echoed, faint and far,
Through distant depths of Heaven it seemed to ring—
For surely such akin to angels are,
Born of the light itself, pure as the Morning Star.

XIV.

Too soon they vanished, passing through the gloom,
And all the waste was silent as before.
Then I beheld three mourners by a tomb:
One bent him down, as in affliction sore,
Crushed to the very earth; another bore
His badge of sorrow flaunting; but the third,
Nor tearful mask nor sable garment wore,
Nor needed to disclose in sign or word
The pain he nursed unseen, the plaint he made unheard.

XV.

But, like a wounded creature, high and low
Directed helpless glances of despair;
With piteous eyes, that wandered to and fro,
As if they fain would plead with earth and air
For ease of anguish too intense to bear;
Till, dimly shaped in the uncertain light,
The lofty Cross stood out before him there!
And all his sinking spirit at the sight
Seemed lifted up to Heaven from gulfs of Death and Night!

XVI.

Then I too hastened onward, knowing well,
Here was a certain refuge from the blast;
Here was a bulwark from the storms of Hell;
Here was the goal of Life attained at last!
Gladly I seized the Cross and held it fast,
While, through the cloud above, a trembling ray
Some pale and gentle star of Mercy cast,
And in my heart I heard an Angel say,
"Poor Child of Sin—behold! thy Sin is washed away!"

XVII.

And lo! beside me stood an aged man,
Wrapped in a palmer's gown of dusky hue;
And down his furrowed cheek a tear-drop ran—
A tear-drop, precious as the morning dew,
A weary soul to freshen and renew.
The while, with reverend arm outstretched, he showed
Far on the dim horizon, scarce in view,
A distant streak of golden light that glowed:
"And there," he said, "is Heaven, and there is thine

XVIII.

"And when thou askest, how this guilt of thine
To such pure realms of glory shall attain?
I answer, none before this Cross divine
Who prayed their hearts out, ever prayed in vain;
And He who hung thereon in mortal pain,
The pangs of shame and anguish freely bore
For such as thee to win immortal gain,
The birthright of thy freedom to restore,
And take thee to Himself—his own for evermore!"

XIX.

"What shall I give Him in return?" I cried,
"Who stooped from Heaven to give his life for me?"
"Give Him thine heart!" the aged man replied;
"One thankful sentence from a bended knee,
One mite in loving homage, offered free,
One cup of water in His name bestowed,
Is all the service He requires from thee.
Farewell! and sometimes think of one who showed
This easy path to Heaven, and set thee on the road!"

XX.

He vanished while he spoke, and in his place,
Behold! a shining Spirit, clad in white,
With bloom of youth eternal on the face,
And in the eyes a lustre calm and bright,
Caught from the fountain of eternal light.
But even as the morning's joyous glow
Seems tempered by remembrance of the Night,
Their glance was softer, deeper, for the woe
Of unforgotten tears, that dimmed them long ago.

XXI.

While pointing upward to the Cross that stood
A grave majestic symbol o'er us there,
The growth and history of its sacred wood,
Predestined in the birth of time to bear
His gracious form, who came to save and spare,
That Spirit told. And every hopeful word
I drank, as hunted creatures drink the air
That brings them life, for all my soul was stirred,
And all my heart went up in worship while I heard.

XXII.

And though the Vision faded out with day,
Though waking to the world it vexed me sore
That all my dream should thus have passed away,
Yet holy fruit the holy lesson bore,
For surely Truth remains for evermore—
Nor, sought in earnest, shall be sought in vain,
Though oft it lies too deep for human lore.
Its sacred purport therefore to explain,
Even as I heard the tale I tell it now again.

BOOK I.

THE SEED.

BOOK I.

THE SEED.

STATELY and sad, the radiant being stands,
Grief on his brow, but vengeance in his hands·
A glorious Angel, vexed by wrath and shame,
A sorrowing Angel, with a sword of flame.
Abashed to meet those eyes of love and scorn,
The sire of countless sinners yet unborn,
First unit, first trangressor of his race,
Bowed in remorse, and, burning with disgrace,
Stoops his imperial head, and veils his stricken face.

The Garden, gorgeous in its maze
    Of flower and fruit, of wood and wold,
A westering sun sets all ablaze,
    In leafy masses tipped with gold ;
Where insect, reptile, bird, and beast,
    In light and warmth, above, below,
The greatest couching by the least,
    Are basking in the evening glow—
Peaceful, as when their Maker scanned
    His creatures in benignant mood,
Surveyed the fabric of his hand,
    And saw that it was good.
While he, but yesterday the lord of all,
His lost dominion wincing to recall,
Can scarce accept the award that bids him roam,
A wanderer, yearning for the gates of home—
Can scarce believe his lot is now to stray,
A hopeless exile, on an aimless way :
No loving hand to guide his steps aright,
Nor daily counsel sought at morning light,

Nor simple, sinless trust, to shelter with by night.
Bitter the thoughts that rankle as they rise,
How easy was the task, how rich the prize!
To mark, unwearied, undepressed by toil,
The generous yield of an unfurrowed soil;
To lip the ready fruit that ripened free,
In lavish clusters on the ungrafted tree;
The herd to count, the docile flock to tend,
In kindly rule, a master and a friend.
No irksome burden this for Man to bear,
The Maker's honour, and the creatures' care;
No grievous impost surely to afford
Love for his charge, obedience to their Lord!
But now, 'tis done! Naught can the past restore
And Eden's gates are shut for evermore.
The one temptation helpless to forego,
The one great secret yearning but to know,
Soiled by the very dust whence he was sprung,
Duped by the woman's hand, the serpent's tongue,
The wrong accepting, while he knew too well

The right—he listened—wavered—ate and fell.
Its work of expiation to begin,
Already waits the penance on the sin.
His mate he blames for her seductive part,
Dethrones her image in his troubled heart,
And half exults, and sorrows half to know
That she who made the trespass, shares the blow
His second self, his love, his life, for him
The cup is filled with sorrow to the brim,
Too deep to mourn aloud, too keen to own.
And thus the Angel speaks in pitying tone,—

 " Blot on our Master's fair design,
  Man, fallen Man, believe
 Sin to record so foul as thine
 The very sons of Light repine,
  Though all unused to grieve.
 Did He not make thee good and great,
  Who raised thee from the dust,
 But little lower in estate
 Than those who, at the golden gate,

In mute obedience watch and wait,
    The servants of His trust!
And shall He not avenge the crime
Hereafter, in the depths of time—
    Of time, that but for thee
Had glided on, a guiltless dream,
Unruffled as a summer stream,
    Into Eternity?
Now, in the round of trouble brought
    By each returning sun,
An expiation must be wrought,
    A daily penance done.
Race after race the doom must share
    In travail, grief, and pain—
The morning task, the nightly care,
    The labour spent in vain;
The longing for a future yet
    Sublimer, purer, higher;
The baffled hope, the weak regret,
    The unfulfilled desire.

THE TRUE CROSS.

The spirit, shrinking back in fear,
    Its homeward path to tread,
Though worn and beaten, smooth and clear,
    By footsteps of the dead,
Or sick and weary, loth to bear
    Its burden to the end—
That, sheltering in a blind despair,
Can court eternal sleep, and dare
    To meet it as a friend,—
Behold! Like watches of the night,
    Age after age shall pass away,
Until the coming of the light,
    The dawning of the day,
When, in a new and wondrous birth,
    Thy race shall be forgiven,
That Love and Peace may reign on earth,
    And perfect Joy in heaven.
Take comfort then, and lift thy head:
    The seed of Her who wrought the woe
Shall bruise the Serpent in his tread.

  Shall heal the sick, and raise the dead,
  Nor scorn to give the hungry bread,
   And—for our Ruler wills it so—
  The doom accepting in their stead,
   Shall ransom all his own below.
Thus, when thy fault its bitter fruit hath borne,
When teem on earth the thistle and the thorn,
When from the tree the leaf must wither sere,
When mildews blight the promise of the year,
When droughts of summer rack the gaping soil,
Or frost of winter robs the fruit of toil,
When in the skies the eagle soars amain
To strike the kid that frolics on the plain,
When o'er the mangled carcase of its dam,
The lordly lion mouths the helpless lamb,
When from a vexed creation, Peace hath fled,
And rest is scarce accorded to the dead—
Their glorious end thy children shall attain,
And find in sorrow, labour, want, and pain,
How suffering grows to joy, and earthly loss to gain.

From dust shall millions rise,
    To dust that shall return,
Whose million souls shall win the immortal prize,
    The immortal wages earn;
And, in each effort of self-sacrifice,
    The immortal lesson learn,
That teaches universal love,
    Compassion for a brother's woe,
Unbounded faith in God above,
    Unshaken trust in man below;
And lowly homage, fain to take
    Example from their Lord and Friend,
To follow in His steps, and make
Their abnegation for His sake,
    Who loved His people to the end.
But for their father's sin,
    The children of thy rescued race
Would never seek the better part to win,
    The higher place—
Could never learn that, wrung from out the soil,

THE SEED.

The yield is but the offspring of the toil;
That patience owes her birth to storm of woes,
And strength from efforts, oft repeated, grows;
That courage, kindling to a danger near,
Sounds but the note of triumph over fear;
And sorrow, training humbled hearts to bear,
Reprieves them on the threshold of despair,
To bid them cry on God, and save themselves by prayer.
 Thus in the womb of every ill,
  Obedient to his Maker's plan,
 A germ of good shall quicken to fulfil
  The destiny of Man.
 Even as the stir and sap of Spring
  From icy Winter shall be born;
 As deepest shades of Night shall bring
  The gleams of Morn—
 So, true to this paternal law.
  The better still shall lurk behind the worse,
 That, smiling up to Mercy, Faith may draw
  A Blessing from a Curse.

Thy heart is sad and weary now,
  Thy step is weak and slow,
Already on thy conscious brow
  Is set the seal of woe.
In gathering glooms of fear and doubt,
  Quenched is thy light;
Blind and forlorn, thou goest out
  Into the night.
But we can stoop from perfect bliss to own
  A brother's part in human guilt and shame,
The holiest angels round the holy throne
  Can pity, while they blame.
For had not we a fallen brother, too?
  Hurled from his place on high—
A brother, beautiful as morning, who
To hopeless strife in wild rebellion flew,
  And writhing now in impotence to die,
Drowns in the gulf of fire, to which he drew
A legion, glorious as our own, while true,
  The Princes of the sky.

Woe to the Dragon! woe to him whose guile
   The banded host of Heaven could thus divide!
Woe to the Serpent! crawling to defile
The woman's heart! Woe to the woman's smile!
     Thine erring guide,
That bade thee fall in folly, weak and vile,
     As angels fell in pride.
And thou art duly punished, and must bear
Through many a grievous year thy load of care,
Fain to be gone, yet hankering to remain,
And half impatient, half inured to pain.
Too jealous of thine own degenerate race
To yield without a pang the Master's place,
While noting, sad and wistful, day by day,
The pride of manhood wasting to decay,
Conscious of blunted senses, dull and dim,
The vigour failing with the falling limb,
The fainting soul, reluctant to depart,
The shrinking stature and the narrowing heart
Till droops the weary head upon the breast,

THE TRUE CROSS.

The closing eye-lids ache to be at rest,
And feeble, fleeting, lost in every breath,
Life only flickers up to welcome Death.
Such is thy penance—Man, it must be so!
Though guiltless spirits share thy guilty woe,
And angels, weeping round the immortal shrine,
Must veil their eyes in grief for thee and thine.
No prayer of ours a pardon yet can gain,
Not all the tears we shed can cleanse the stain.
A holier price thy trespass must recall,
More sacred drops on thy behalf shall fall ;
I tremble while I speak, I dare not tell thee all.
Behold, poor outcast lingering by the gate,
In memory of repentance found too late,
In token of the trespass and the tree,
Seeds of its fatal fruit, I offer, three.
The gift I charge thee all thy life to save,
And bid thy children plant it on thy grave.
So, in the fulness of appointed time,
When shoots the sacred sapling to its prime,

That mystic growth shall surely serve to trace,
Age after age, the story of thy race.
In all its varying turns of fortune share,
To chance, and change, a faithful witness bear,
Remain, itself uninjured by decay,
While shifting nations fade and pass away,
To mark how growth of evil, once begun,
Takes wider scope, bequeathed from sire to son,
Till Mercy, weary of the hopeless strife,
Unclasps her hands to plead no more for life,
And darker, deeper, closing deadlier in,
A waste of waters hides a world of sin.
Yet shall a chosen few the judgment fly,
Nor all thy children thus be doomed to die,
And in the Ark that floats them safe and fair,
A plank from that strange tree the freight shall bear
Preserving and preserved, the gulf to span,
To bridge the coming history of Man.
Thereafter, planted in a Southern land,
With fresher leaf, and growth renewed to stand,

Shall screen a patriarch's tent upon the plains,
And shade the angel-guests he entertains.
Its task not yet fulfilled, again shall feel
The rasping malice of the limber steel,
Cut, planed, and deftly fashioned to a board
That roofs in pride the Temple of the Lord.
Enriched with golden plate and clamp and ring
To crown the wisdom of the wisest king;
Thence, in a day of vengeance, wrath and woe,
Torn down and trampled by a foreign foe,
When Judah's warrior turns in shameful flight
To mark his Lion, worsted in the fight;
When heathens, raging in their godless ire,
The holy places waste with sword and fire,
Stripped of its wealth, denuded of its state,
Polluting hands shall thrust it from the gate,
Hurling the charred and blackened beam to cool
And rot, neglected in Bethesda's pool,
For ages in those shallows to remain,
Half-bare, and half-submerged—but not in vain,

THE SEED.

For soon the troubled waters shall reveal
Its virtue, conscious of their power to heal,
And soon, distorted figures, warped and wrung,
The aching limb, the swoln and palsied tongue,
The halt, the maimed, the blind—a suffering band,
At stated hours shall round the margin stand,
With pale and eager faces, fain to prove
The cure, and, watching till the surface move,
Await the turn that bids their anguish cease,
Wash and be clean—and so depart in peace!
 Yet light of day once more to meet,
  In cruel shape the beam shall stand
 Its expiation to complete,
  Its victim to demand.
I see a wild and tossing crowd,
 I see it break in angry waves
Around an eagle-standard, proud
 To flaunt above a race of slaves.
I see a priest with garments rent,
 I see a warrior bright in mail,

I see, with pain and labour bent,
A patient figure, worn and spent,
   A face resigned and pale,—
A scarlet robe in mocking state,
   In savage jest a crown of thorn.
And up the street, and by the gate,
Through all that malice can create,
Of scoff and jeer, and stormy hate,
While Manhood sinks beneath the weight,
   God's Cross of Ransom borne.
Enough! I veil mine eyes in awe,
   In horror, wrath, and shame,
Nor dare I question his decree, whose law
Forbids the Legions of his Host to draw
   Their swords of flame,
And flying earthward, urged by holy ire,
To cleanse in blood, and purify with fire,
   The honour of his name.
But He who drives the wanderer out to-day,
Whose will to save, exceeds his power to slay;

Whose mercy ever leans to pardon first,
Who suffers long the vilest and the worst,
For thee and thine hath store of pity still,
And bids thee trust him yet through good and ill:
Else had his angel never dared to trace
The wondrous future of thine erring race,
Predestined in the pangs of mortal strife
To win their heir-ship of immortal life.
And now the doom is read, the tale is told,
The volume of the mighty plan unrolled:
A crime—a curse—a forfeit and a loss—
A gain—a hope—a ransom and a cross.
For thee the lines are drawn, the lot is cast,
Before thee lies the Future—on the Past,
Poor child of sorrow, turn, and look thy loving last!'

  The words were yet upon his tongue
  When back the flashing portals swung,
   The gates of fire and gold.
  On this our earth hath never been
  So fair a sight as lay between,

Nor eye of man hath ever seen,
　　Nor speech of man hath told,
Nor mind of man conceived in all its lore,
Such marvels as one glimpse of Eden bore.
　　The world without was dark and bare,
　　　　A shadowy waste of gloom and sin,
　　But streams of lustre filled the air,
　　　　A flood of glory shone within—
It came direct from Him, whose might
　　Had wisely planned and fashioned all
It knew no change of day and night,
　　It could not cease, nor fade, nor pall,
It bathed the sward in dazzling white,
It hung the tree with jewels bright,
Its very dews were drops of light
　　From heaven that seemed to fall.
And in the midst, with silver spray
　　That, like a living thing at play,
Shot upward in the face of day,
　　A fountain, crystal-clear,

> Leapt, laughed, and sparkled in its mirth
> To four great streams while giving birth,
> That watered all the bounds of earth,
> > And took their rise from here.

Beside it stood a mighty tree and tall,
Stripped of its bark, with foliage in the fall,
For round its trunk, in many a writhing fold,
A Serpent clung—that Serpent wise and old,
Who, gathering venom through the peaceful time,
Had spotted God's own garden with his slime.
About him, shrunk the leaf, and paled the fruit,
Below, the unpoisoned tree struck healthier root,
In pointed fibres, sharpening as they grew,
To pierce his coils, and stab him through and through;
Yet, while he curled in anguish well concealed,
His sleek and subtle head no sign of pain revealed.

> Bewildered, horror struck, to gaze
> > On sight so awful, thus unrolled,
> The exile stood in blank amaze,
> Till now the Angel bade him raise

His eyes yet greater marvels to behold,
And looking upward see,
With branches spreading wide and free,
The stately summit of that mystic tree
   Its leaves in Heaven unfold.
With richer growth expanding in the air,
Bud, fruit and flower uniting, fresh and fair,
As though in lavish yield rejoiced to fling
Its wealth of Autumn o'er its hopes of Spring.
While through the bowers of green, with blossoms
    graced,
With twining shoot and tendril interlaced,
Soft, pure and white as flakes of falling snow,
Seven gentle doves were flitting to and fro;
A simple music murmuring, sad and sweet,
In strains they never wearied to repeat,
On restless pinion wheeling, fain to bring
Unceasing homage to their Infant-King.
   For on that tree so good and fair,
    So garnished in a wealth untold,

Of all it promised, all it bare,
  The richest fruit behold!
Brighter than dawn, and undefiled
  As morning's opening ray,
A living babe—a holy child,
  More beautiful than day!
And while the seven doves were winging
  Seven circles round its head,
Seven stars, their lustre flinging,
Seven spirits, praises singing
  Watched about the bed
Whereon that Infant lay reclining,
  Tended by the hands of One,
Pure as gold beyond refining,
Clad in raiment white and shining,
  Dazzling like the sun—
A Woman of a gracious port and eye,
Kind as the earth, and comely as the sky.
  She stooped her brow, serene and fair,
    To look upon the Child.

And wound her arms about him there
With all a mother's helpful care,
And half in pride, and half in prayer,
 She blessed him when he smiled.
The love between that holy twain
 Was more of heaven than earth;
A mother's love conceived in pain,
By faith sublimed, to entertain
Belief in His eternal reign
 To whom its pangs gave birth,
Nor yet in earthly sorrows to forego
Its earthly part of suffering, fear, and woe.
Enraptured in a trance of mute delight,
Long gazed the outcast on that goodly sight,
While tears of grateful hope and sweet surprise
Swelled at his heart, and mounted to his eyes.
In sullen mood, he had but thought as yet
The forfeit, not the trespass, to regret.
Till now, a true repentance to begin,
The sense of pardon taught the shame of sin;

Roused a remorse, existent, though it slept,
And thus his conscience smote him—and he wept.
The Angel marked that mien so altered now,
And brighter shone the star upon his brow,
For well the gentle, pitying spirit knew
That watered thus, the plant of Mercy grew,
And man unfriended, faltering on the way,
Must learn to weep before he learns to pray.
With hands out-stretched, his glorious head he bent,
And smiled a brother's love, and blessed him as he went
In part consoled, though loth to leave the place,
Our erring father, with dejected face,
Turned from his home behind those gates of light,
And journeyed forth a wanderer through the night;
To learn, like all his race, that in the strife
Of good with evil, called by mortals, life,
These, for a future destined, must forego
Their share in all they prize the most below.
Each human heart must bear the human test,
And yield to God the love it loves the best.

So shall it rise, the better part to own,
And anchoring earthly hope on heaven alone,
Shall purge immortal ore from mortal dross,
To win a priceless gain in paltry loss.
Nor yet shall common kindly joys forego,
But greet them lightly as they come and go,
With placid trust accepting smile and frown,
Exalted not by this, nor yet by that cast down.
As one to welcome Summer's golden hours,
Who sows a cultured plot with garden flowers,
Can laugh if early frost destroy the shoots,
Or brutal malice pluck them by the roots,
Because, though now the space be spoiled and clear,
Well doth he know that in the coming year
His hands can raise a coming crop; but he
Who on his ground elects to plant a tree,
Had need preserve its deeper growth with care,
For lo! the earth uptorn, the place laid bare,
Must henceforth mock the toil he plies in vain,
And on that spot the flowers shall never bloom again!

Thus human love that strikes too deep a root,
In human lives shall bear a poisoned fruit,
And when, the laws of Wisdom to obey,
Those plants of Folly must be plucked away,
So tangled is the growth, so keen the smart,
To rend the fibres surely breaks the heart.
But man, in darkest hour of need and pain,
Shall never seek for aid and ease in vain ;
A gentle balm, a soothing salve shall find
In deeds of mercy offered to his kind ;
With sweet compassion lifting those that fall,
Excusing, pitying, helping, loving all.
Thus to absorb in other's woes his own,
Thus for another's errors to atone,
And—since to trip in trespass is to live—
Learn from his God the lesson—to forgive.
So Adam, half unmindful of his fate,
Turned in relenting mood to seek his mate,
Marked the dim shape that followed in the gloom,
And loved her better for their common doom.

He stretched a clinging hand to meet
   A clinging hand that met his own,
Nor ceased, nor wearied to repeat
The tender words of solace sweet,
   She answered with a moan;
For, sharper than a thrust of steel,
It stabs a woman's heart to feel
   In self-reproachful pain,
How from the head she loves the best—
The head that shelters in her breast—
   She strives to ward in vain
Storms that her own great error has brought down,
Yet finds a smile where she had feared a frown.
   He drew her closer, closer yet,
     To comfort and to cheer.
   Her touch was cold, her cheek was wet,
     She never seemed so dear,
   And, like a child that shrinks from harm,
   She wrapped her in his circling arm,
   And silent, pleaded all the charm

Of weakness and of fear.
Thus side by side, and hand in hand,
    They passed together through the night—
Before them loomed a shadowy land,
    Behind them waned a sinking light,
Yet calm and hopeful, though subdued,
    They journeyed on the uncertain way.
Each in the other's altered mood
Saw love renewing and renewed,
    While each was fain to say,
" Though dark the hour, the labour rude,
For hearts with mutual hopes imbued,
There smiles a future to be wooed,
    There dawns a coming day!
Then reunited, trusting as at first,
Shall we not share the best, as we can dare the worst!"
    And so their burden, each for each
        They lightened, while they bore
    The loveliest lesson, thus to teach
        Of all our human lore.

For he who thinks to stand alone,
    Alone shall surely fall—
Our very woes are not our own,
    But held in trust for all.
The bitter tears that secret flow,
    In solitary pain,
May freshen other lives, although
Our barren hopes can never know
    Their fertilizing rain ;
And we who work, and we who weep,
    Nor weep nor work in vain,
If other hands our harvest reap,
And other hearts with joy shall leap
    To garner up our grain.

The wanderers journeyed many an hour,
Nor staid for rest by brake nor bower—
It seemed as though some hidden power,
    Or instinct at the least,
Born of their own imperious need,

That yearned for light their steps to lead,
Impelled them onward to proceed,
   And drove them to the East.
Till, for his mate, with labour spent,
He paused a little space, and bent
His stately head to her, who leant
   Her own upon his breast,
And turned, and bade her mark how fair
The Garden slept behind them, there:
How still the tree—how soft the air
   In calm and hush of rest,
And how, retiring, pale, and proud,
The Moon, as in a silver shroud,
Dimmed by a streak of dappled cloud,
   Went down into the west.

She marked it all, and marked beside
   On that beloved brow,
The bitter shame it strove to hide,
The scorn of self, the wounded pride

THE TRUE CROSS.

That marred its grandeur now,
And drew him to their destined way,
   And urged him not in vain.
And pointed where before them lay
The promise of approaching day,
A pale and narrow seam of grey,
   Yet level with the plain ;
A scanty rift that widened fast,
In token night was surely past,
And joyous morning come at last
   To gladden earth again.
He found a comfort in the thought,
A comfort by the Woman brought.
   Yet little had availed
Without that hopeful, helpful guide,
Strength, wisdom, fortitude, and pride,
   When all the Man had failed!
Now, like the children of his race,
God's future he was armed to face,
   With Life prepared to cope ;

For, broken, baffled, and bereft,
Those are not wholly lost whose hearts have left
A Memory and a Hope.

BOOK II.

THE ARK.

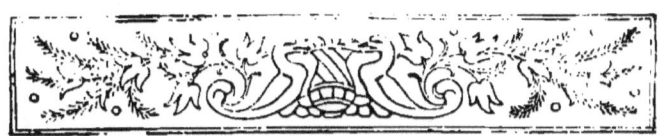

BOOK II.

THE ARK.

CANTO I.

I.

BEHOLD the mountain towering in its pride,
With russet robe, and crown of ruddy gold,
And shaggy fringe of copses crimson-dyed
Beneath the glows of sunset, and behold
The great primeval landscape all unrolled
In grandeur of design, though wild and rude.
The gorgeous hues, the outline free and bold,
Unbridled torrent, and impervious wood,
The wilderness untamed. The world before the Flood!

II.

Where mighty monsters roamed, that have to-day
Nor like nor kindred here.   The enormous bear,
In deep recess of rocky cave that lay,
Yet made in deep recess a shallow lair.
The ungainly mammoth, coarse with matted hair,
A bulky mass, but half informed with life;
Yet from his torpor roused, should hunters dare
Provoke his sloth, a foe with fury rife,
No unresisting prey in that gigantic strife.

III.

And wingless birds that grovelled on the earth,
Half-bird, half-reptile.   Such as it would seem
To freak of nature owed abortive birth.
And creatures mis-begotten of the stream,
In hideous shapes, fantastic as a dream,
When in a trance the sleeper's fears prevail,
And shadowy horror quenches reason's gleam,
Formed but a lewd and loathsome length to trail,
And score the yielding slime with armour-plated scale.

IV.

And there was beauty, such as not since then
Hath shone on earth to dazzle earthly eye.
Beauty! that worn by daughters but of men,
Could yet disturb the councils of the sky,
And draw God's very children down to die.
And there was strength colossal, such as reared
A race of Giants, stubborn, proud, and high—
A daring race, that neither hoped nor feared,
Regarded naught on earth, nor aught in heaven revered.

V.

For wild the dreams of passion that had been
In those wild mountains, when the world was young.
When sons of God, their nature to demean,
Consumed with longing, yet with anguish wrung,
Their starry crowns to earthly idols flung,
Their snowy robes in earthly mire defiled,
Duped by the loving glance, the flattering tongue,
Exulting, even thus betrayed, beguiled—
Lured from their high estate because a woman smiled.

VI.

Sweet were the tortures of the summer night,
The rapture of suspense, and more than sweet
The agony of joy and fierce delight,
That bade her wind about the Vision's feet,
And upward writhe his scorching clasp to meet.
But bitter was the end, and keen the smart
(Such oft-told tale it boots not to repeat),
For still the doom is shared when lovers part—
One bears a broken faith, and one a broken heart.

VII.

Then were there stricken faces, vexed and pale,
That through the waste went flitting here and there,
Like phantoms seeking rest without avail,
And haggard eyes, and backward-streaming hair,
And hands outstretched to heaven in wild despair.
While ever swelled and sank and swelled again,
A piteous wail that quivered in the air,
A woeful music set to fitful strain,
The dirge of buried hopes, and love that loved in vain.

VIII.

Yet hence arose a fierce imperious race,
Of glorious beauty and gigantic frame,
Who owed their demon-strength, their angel-face,
To link of heavenly guilt and earthly shame,
With holier natures kindred who could claim,
But felt for holier natures haughty scorn;
Inviting evil, courting hate and blame—
Stern with the proud, yet trampling the forlorn,
And still inflicting wrong on all of Woman born.

IX.

Insatiate in a mad desire of strife,
A thirst for danger, and a wild delight
To take at every turn, or peril—life.
Exulting in the triumph of their might,
Yet loving less the victory than the fight.
To fear unable and untaught to spare,
Rejoicing to pursue, by day and night,
Huge beasts of chase, the mammoth or the bear,
And track the monster home, and slay him in his lair.

X.

Bathed in a crimson glow of eventide,
The crimson glow that flooded all the west,
There stood a figure on the mountain-side,
In scanty garments of the hunter dressed,
With sinewy limbs and mighty bulk of chest,
Tall, strong, and fair, a comely child of sin,
Yet of his race the gentlest and the best,
And at his feet there lay a monster's skin.
Well was that hunter formed, such dangerous spoil to win.

XI.

For in the combat he was fierce and strong,
Though kind and courteous when the strife was done.
Wassail and wine he loved, and mirth and song,
Nor smile of woman scorned, though lightly won
In sumptuous banquet, spread at set of sun.
A nature prone to pleasure, prompt to ire,
Impatient of the curb, not suffering long
Restraint, reproof, nor check to its desire,
For through that earthly mould there coursed unearthly fire.

XII.

Brief was his pause of contemplation there,
For soon, to rouse his keen and practised ear,
Broke on the stillness of the summer air
A ring of tools, repeated quick and clear.
Plank-tearing plane and hammer he could hear,
And rasping saw that grated in and out,
As when some wooden fabric workmen rear
　With toil and craft.　Not long he stood in doubt,
But gathered up his spoil, and went to seek it out.

XIII.

Descending swift the mountain's rugged side,
He bounded down, the wished-for spot to gain.
With light and airy tread, but sweeping stride,
Like some good courser scouring o'er the plain,
That meets in managed leap the mastering rein.
With such good courser's strength and speed endowed,
Like him he halted—short, as in disdain,
　And flung his head aloft with gesture proud,
And stood at gaze, and laughed, in laughter long and loud.

XIV.

For lo! the framework of a vast design,
Now verging on completion, met his eye,
Adjusted well with plummet, scale, and line,
Lest bulwark, beam, or joist should fit awry,
Warped from the seemly level, fair and high,
Of timbers, cornered, each in other's niche.
And, though the wood was seasoned now, and dry,
Its porous grain to strengthen and enrich
By wise preventive care, pitched in and out with pitch.

XV.

One thoughtful head the great device had planned,
Eight brawny arms the unceasing labour plied;
For, clothed in strength of willing heart and hand,
Four goodly men were working side by side:
Three in the comely prime of manhood's pride,
The fourth with reverend brows and beard of grey,
Whose wisdom all the master-craft supplied,
Instructing these his sons, each piece to lay.
Behests of such a sire, well might such sons obey!

XVI.

The youngest-born was comely, tall and spare,
Or tool or weapon deftly formed to ply,
With ruddy cheek, and wealth of golden hair,
And gentle mien, and features calm and high;
The next seemed swarthier, tanned by sunnier sky,
With bulky limbs, and chest more squarely made;
The third, whose keener face and narrower eye
A fine and subtle sense of skill conveyed,
The shrewd constructive power in every glance betrayed.

XVII.

Ceaseless had been their toil from break of day,
Nor ceased their toil when day was nearly done,
For dark prophetic fear forbade delay,
And coming need of work long since begun,
Impelled to ceaseless effort sire and son—
That coming need though all the world ignored,
Persistent its unbridled course to run,
Provoking vengeance, soon to be out-poured,
And still devising sins of heaven and earth abhorred.

XVIII.

For this, the skies were heavy with a curse,
Ere long to wash pollution from the land.
Man's thought was evil now, his action worse,
Black was the heart, and red the ruthless hand,
And foul the fires by guilt and passion fanned.
Untamed their wild rebellion, who could dare
The Maker's laws to challenge and withstand,
Of pardon unconcerned, unblessed by prayer,
The doom to turn aside, that trembled in the air.

XIX.

Yet could eternal Mercy set apart
One righteous nature from the unrighteous crew.
A man of blameless life, and spotless heart,
With pious precepts stored. A man who knew,
And practised, godly ways, and taught them too.
For him and his the judgment could suspend,
In purpose to preserve that chosen few,
Their needs to help, their weakness to defend,
Bestow them in its care, and keep them to the end.

XX.

So, while his erring brethren ate and drank,
Married and gave in marriage, as they would;
Their souls in vile pollution steeped and sank,
And chose the evil while they saw the good—
The tide of life's corruption he withstood,
Sought the deep silence of the forest-glade,
To commune with himself in solitude,
And on behalf of friends and kindred made
Oblation to his God, and wept, and knelt, and prayed.

XXI.

Nor did his God forget him, in the gloom
And stillness of the woods, but stooped to lend
A gracious ear, and warned him of the doom,
And spoke, as speaks a mortal with his friend,
Vouchsafing partial pardon to extend,
Nor scorned to teach him how to plan and make
An ark, his charge to shelter and defend,
For of each living thing he bade him take
A sample to survive, and spared them for his sake.

XXII.

Thus while the wise directions he obeyed,
And searched the forest diligently through,
He found a goodly giant of the glade—
So vast of girth, so stately, that he knew
(For old tradition pointed where it grew)
How Seth had seen those budding branches wave,
And Enos spared the growth, himself should hew.
For that great tree, up-towering fair and brave,
Struck deep its ancient root in Adam's ancient grave.

XXIII.

With brandished axe he brought it to the ground,
And carved a mighty beam from out its heart—
A mighty beam, hereafter to be found
The strength sustaining of its strongest part,
In all the floating fabric of his art;
And girded it with iron, to afford
Supporting power, lest it should strain or start,
And in its veins the seething resin poured,
And proved it firm and sound by smiting on the board.

XXIV.

As at his forge in red relief and glow,
A smith, with salient muscles, shoulder-bare,
Completes his hearty labour, blow by blow—
So, tinged with crimson of the evening air,
This master-workman, striking just and fair,
His master-strokes repeated on the wood,
Nor trouble seemed to grudge, nor toil to spare,
But spent his strength, and laboured all he could;
Therefore the giant laughed in no ungentle mood.

XXV.

"Old man!" said he, "what boots it thus to slave?
Were it not wise the fruitless task to leave,
And join with us, the idle, gay, and brave,
Who love the chase at noon, the feast at eve
Who in our weapons and ourselves believe?
Thine seems a long endurance, little worth,
An endless labour, hopeless of reprieve.
Come then, and cheer thy heart with wine and mirth;
These are the gifts of heaven, and these the joys of earth.

XXVI.

"Nor are they far to seek. For now behold
The ready banquet, set in order fair
With dainty meats and brimming cups of gold.
Laughter and song, and joyous hearts are there,
And smiling women with their sun-bright hair;
Nor these brave youths shall linger here the while.
I welcome all! Then nothing stint nor spare.
For thee the cup; for them bright woman's smile
The lagging hours of night shall sweeten and beguile.

XXVII.

"Such are the gods that heaven and earth subdue,
Such are the gods we worship, for we know
Their rights the strength and courage shall renew
That scorn to shrink from aught above, below,
Nor yield to mortal nor immortal foe.
Rouse then thy failing heart with mirth and wine;
So shall the mounting pulses leap and glow,
While manhood all its forces shall combine
To trample human might and beard the power divine!

XXVIII.

" To-morrow in the flush of morning's pride,
Together will we fare, a laughing band,
Our joyous measure treading side by side,
Our voices blending—linking hand in hand,
To fire these goodly timbers where they stand ;
Sweet incense then shall pitch and resin raise,
Homage from him who worked to him who planned—
Forsooth, a pious offering all a-blaze!
Said I not well?   Old man, thou shrinkest in amaze!"

XXIX.

But he whom thus the haughty youth addressed,
Across laborious brows his garment drew,
And paused a space of no unwelcome rest,
Though vexed and sad his thoughtful visage grew,
As one who feared the future he fore-knew,
Its gathering cloud of evil loth to scan,
So many that should compass, spare so few ;
When, in accordance with its Maker's plan,   [man.
The Earth should sink engulfed, borne down by sins of

XXX.

"These are the gods ye worship!" he repeated
"False gods! false worship! falsest trick of all,
By such delusive idols to be cheated!
How shall ye look when on your gods ye call
In stress of need, the bravest to appal?
When upward still the avenging waters glide,
And downward still the avenging waters fall,
And woman's pliant grace, man's stalwart pride,
Are borne like wisps of weed, waifs on the mounting tide.

XXXI.

"When, blinded by the green encircling wave,
The baffled mother, choking in despair,
Shall toss her arms aloft, her babe to save,
Launched to the dwindling peak of granite, where
The tigress licks her cubs, with famished glare,
And grating claws that cling in slippery hold,
Yet couches to await the prey; but ere
That reeking breath the living child enfold,
Lo! the dead woman sinks through waters deep and cold!

XXXII.

" While all around with bloated corpses rife,
A wrecked creation spots the heaving deep:
Some lifted upward, dance, as mocking life,
Some through the veiling surface loathsome peep,
And still the cruel waters laugh and leap.
How fare your brethren now, the strong, the brave?
Call on your gods aloud! and bid them keep
Their children from the rolling ruthless wave—
Call on your gods, I say! Your gods that cannot save!

XXXIII.

" On *my* God will I call. On him rely
Whose laws I love, and in his truth confide.
To safety shall he waft me fair and high;
Nor counsel shall withhold my course to guide,
Borne on the flow of that resistless tide,
Which shall not ebb, nor dwindle, nor abate,
Till you and yours have foundered in your pride—
Swamp'd, with the brutes to perish small and great.
Will ye not turn in time? It is not yet too late!"

XXXIV.

Loud laughed the giant. "Dotard! fool!" he said;
"But that it rouses mirth such tales to hear,
My wrath had sure descended on his head
Who in my presence dares to mention fear,
Or hint I value danger, far or near.
The deeps may rise—I'll bale them in my shield!
The skies may fall—I'll prop them on my spear!
Worse can I dare than thou hast thus revealed,
Yet scorn from Fate to flinch—to God refuse to yield!

XXXV.

"And if it come to pass, these words of thine
Hereafter are fulfilled, remember thou
No whit I shrank from power nor wrath divine,
Nor 'bated aught of what I tell thee now.
While planted firm on solid earth, I vow,
That if but one square inch of standing-room
This curse of spreading waters shall allow,
Engulfed and sinking in that yielding tomb,
Thy God will I abjure, and dare his instant doom!"

XXXVI.

Once more he laughed, and scornful strode away,
Nor paused for that concerned and sorrowing face,
So fain to bid him ponder yet and stay,
As though already, ere he left the place,
In sad prophetic instinct it could trace
Pale fires of doom about the comely head,
So comely, yet so proud, like all his race;
Could mark the faded eyes, their lustre fled,
The gallant beauty marred, for ever lost and dead.

XXXVII.

Grieving, one ceased from toil with fall of night;
The while to eat the fat, and drink the strong,
Gay with his boast, exulting in his might,
The other sped those forest-glades along,
Guided by clash of cups and burst of song,
That bade him to the joyous feast repair.
With notes of mirth that to such scenes belong,
High rose the tide of revel, free and fair,
And torches flashed and streamed, to redden all the air.

XXXVIII.

There were the cups that glow, the gems that gleam,
And glorious women with their hair unbound,
And lovely faces, lustrous as a dream,
And snowy, shapely arms, gold-girded round.
Bright were their looks and smiles, and sweet the sound
Of those soft voices rippling round the board;
And each had lost a heart, and each had found
The loss supplied a master and a lord,
Whom for a space she loved, and while she loved, adored.

XXXIX.

For Woman then was fond, as Woman now,
When Man is less heroic than of yore.
Deep was her wit, though calm and smooth her brow;
Deep was her heart, and tender to the core,
Ungrudging all its treasure to out-pour
At those dear feet she worshipped for a while.
Yet, changing once, she changed for evermore,
And, fain to lure fresh captives in her smile,
Still a fresh triumph found, fresh lovers to beguile.

XL.

By that proud youth, of all the women there
The proudest and the loveliest sat her down;
Bright were her glances, on her forehead fair
The glory of her tresses wreathed a crown,
And jewels looped her hair and looped her gown.
Yet when he spoke she scarcely bent to hear,
Nor much she seemed to heed with smile or frown,
But in her eyes there came the lovelight clear,
That shone for him alone—the loved one, whispering near.

XLI.

And now she blushed and trembled with delight,
And now she stumbled in her speech, and sighed,
And longed, in coolness of the outer night,
On that broad breast her burning brow to hide,
Alone with *him*, her treasure and her pride.
For here were noise and glare, and laughter rang,
Till gaily on her name some reveller cried.
Then ceased the tongues to wag, the cups to clang,
And sank the din of mirth to silence while she sang.

"I weep and watch—I weep and wait,
He cometh not—he cometh late—
My lord, my love, mine angel-mate,
    Thou tarriest long!
My heart is humble now and meek,
My heart is full, I needs must speak,
My heart is sad and sore and weak,
    But love is strong.
And ringeth in my brain its knell,
    Farewell! Farewell!
Thy kiss yet burneth on my brow,
The burning kiss that sealed thy vow—
My lord hath ceased to love me now—
    I make my moan.
Oh! joy when heart on heart could beat!
Oh! madness when our lips could meet!
Come back, and I will kiss thy feet!
    My King! my own!
Come back! I pray—beseech—implore!
    Once more—once more!
Will he not hear me? Yes—behold

The mist of stars—the shine of gold!
His wings are round me as of old.
  Oh! vision vain!
To mock my longing, loving sight,
One instant with its flood of light,
Then fade in deepest dark of night,
  Nor rise again.
How hard to bear, tongue cannot tell!
  Farewell—Farewell—
   Farewell!"

XLII.

Died the sweet voice away in trembling tone,
Yet lingered in the hearts of those who heard,
And bade them know its sadness for their own;
While each, with choking throat and vision blurred,
Felt all the finer chords of nature stirred.
Though one alone she valued o'er the rest
Nor look of love betrayed, nor uttered word,
But stole a seeking hand to hers, and pressed
The kind and clinging hand, that answered, thus caressed.

XLIII.

And so they passed in cruel joys the day,
So drank and shouted through the calm of night,
In scorn of that just man, who bade them stay
Their reddened hands, their ruthless, reckless might,
Although his work was daily in their sight—
Accomplished now through toil of many a year
Exulting all his warning to requite
With unbelieving jest, and flout, and jeer.
And thus they lived and laughed, and thus the end drew near.

XLIV.

Till one still night there stole upon the breeze
A mournful whisper, troubling all the air,
As though a spirit moaned among the trees,
And prayed for rest with piteous pleading prayer,
Reproachful of the boisterous revellers there.
Each looked enquiring in the other's eyes,
And each returned the other's wistful stare,
Or smiled, a grim foreboding to disguise,
And set the goblet down and listened in surprise.

XLV.

Soon was the riddle read, and broke the spell,
For like a pelt of stones by slingers cast,
Drop following drop, that widened as they fell,
Each larger, heavier, angrier than the last,
The hissing storm descended, thick and fast.
On night's dark brow there came a darker frown,
Rose the wild whisper to a wilder blast,
While, insect, flower, and fruit to drench and drown,
Poured from the blackening skies great sheets of water down.

XLVI.

Then Woman's eye dilated, paled her cheek,
And Man his brow uplifted, bold and high,
As fain in heaven or earth his foe to seek—
The foe in heaven or earth he would defy.
Whom shall he dread who dreadeth not to die?
And wrung by fear, again and yet again
There broke from gentle hearts a stifled cry,
While these in horror, those in fierce disdain,
Laughed — shouted — whispered — scoffed —" Behold!

CANTO II.

I.

THE rain—the rain. In ceaseless, silent fall
   It varied not nor stinted day by day,
   Wove o'er the soaking earth its misty pall,
And blurred the landscape in a shroud of grey,
Uncheered, unbroken by a rift or ray.
Loomed in the haze gigantic, rock and tree,
On wood and hill thick folds of vapour lay,
   Bubbled the spring, the fountain spouted free,
And streams to rivers swelled, and rivers to a sea.

II.

A dim grey sea, that covered all the plain,
By peak and islet studded here and there,
Thronged with a swarm of living creatures, fain
On each dry spot for refuge to repair.
Great beasts of field and forest, birds of air,
Scared by a watery world, a watery sky,
That looked to heaven in silent pleading prayer,
And turned on earth a solemn, seeking eye;
And flocked, and roamed, and roared, and shivered, loth to die.

III.

For while the narrowing island dwindled fast,
And while the widening waters swelled and rose,
By press of common need together cast,
Tamed by a common danger, crowded those
Whose habits in their freedom made them foes.
Yet did the stronger push the weak aside,
While inward still the remnant sought to close,
Till came the mastering flood o'er all to glide,
And bore the conqueror off, and swamped him in its tide

IV.

Some wrestled hard, ere yielding thus to die,
And some without an effort sank outright;
Some drowned with angry snort and bubbling cry,
And some struck out and swam with all their might,
By nature's instinct urged, for life to fight.
In dumb and dogged hope that sought to gain
The distant upland, hidden from their sight,
Their failing strength to rack, their limbs to strain,
And struggle blindly on, but struggle on in vain.

V.

Each higher mountain pass ere now was thronged
With mighty moving creatures from below,
Whose short sharp cry, or dismal howl prolonged,
The fierce suspicion of a lurking foe,
And sense of coming danger, seemed to show
While, undetected yet of eye or ear;
With stealthy gait they traversed to and fro,
Or thundering up and down in wild career,
Pushed, worried, fought, and gored, in anger and in fear.

VI.

For while destruction threatened from afar,
Destruction none the less was close at hand.
In every thicket lurked the insidious war,
By man called sport, that man's device had planned
To sweep his game, God's creatures, from the land.
Nor wanton wounds nor death he spared to deal,
Nor size nor strength his cunning could withstand,
That bade the mammoth in its death-pang reel,
And to the cave-bear's heart drove home the quivering steel.

VII.

The lordly race that slaughter loved so well,
Because the waters covered all below,
On loftier mountains now were fain to dwell,
Exulting in vain-glorious boast to know
What gallant herds those wooded heights could show—
Great monsters, worthy of the days of yore,
Such as their fathers hunted long ago.
And since the rain had fall'n, they laughed and swore
The chase was nobler, livelier, deadlier than before.

VIII.

At peaceful morning-tide they rose to slay,
With noisy revel scared the hush of night;
Man's fiercer instincts prompted to obey,
In wine and wassail took a wild delight.
Great human hearts rejoicing in their might,
Yet conscious of a calm resistless power,
That still refused to spare and scorned to fight;
That, day by day, caused darker skies to lower,
And bade the creeping flood gain on them, hour by hour.

IX.

But yet they took nor heed nor warning, knew
No worship but their own unholy will.
A fearless, ruthless, reckless, godless crew,
In time of wrath predestined to fulfil
The award of Him who did but threaten still,
Whose vengeance in each cloud although they saw,
Heard in each breeze that moaned about the hill,
Nor shame nor fear they owned, nor shrank in awe,
God's precepts to ignore, and break man's sterner law.

X.

And now behold, as heretofore revealed
By one inspired who preached to all the rest,
The fountains of the mighty deep unsealed,
Great tidal waves that mounted unrepressed,
Dark—shining—edged with white and ragged crest,
That wrapped the hills in their embraces cold—
Hills that should sink and perish, thus caressed;
That drove each living thing from hold to hold,
And upward seethed and surged, and onward roared and rolled.

XI

Thus for each cubit's breadth of standing-room,
Imperious Man was now compelled to strive
With brutes, the dumb companions of his doom;
Fain from their nook the monster-cubs to drive,
And save his own weak shivering babes alive.
Till some fierce mother that he thought to slay
Would rise in her despair to rend and rive,
When, grappling in the base inglorious fray,
The impartial waters came and swept them both away.

XII.

Yet, like the autumn fruit in mellow skies,
That drops mature and noiseless from the tree,
These lordly natures, with defiant eyes,
Sank stern and silent in the silent sea.
While earth remained, they laughed and revelled free,
When earth was gone, they wrapped them in their pride
Untamed in this the last extremity;
Looked scornful up to heaven, then turned aside,
And set their dogged teeth, and cursed their God, and died.

XIII.

While, if some lowlier spirit seemed to cower,
And shrank to meet the phantom, face to face,
That scared its senses in this darker hour,
Tradition and inherent pride of race
Taught such a late repentance was disgrace.
Who but a coward would recall the past?
Or hope in death, life's journey to retrace?
Behold! the sin was sinned, the lot was cast!
Together would they sink, together drown at last!

XIV.

Fenced in a cleft of rock, remote and high,
Like sea-birds sheltering from the stormy air,
Perched on some ledge of granite, smooth and dry,
Behold ensconced aloft a lonely pair!
One who had heard the prophet's pleading prayer,
Yet scorned the voice prophetic to obey,
And one who lured him here in tender care,
And scarce acknowledged hope that for a day
The doom she might suspend—the judgment thus delay.

XV.

And these had loved each other with a love,
Though born of earth, and earthly in its kind,
Yet tinged with holier lustre from above,
The fair and chastened ray of heaven, designed
To lead us up to light, however blind.
For those who, in their lives, one single grain
Of pure and true affection have refined,
And wrung from viler dross through grief and pain,
Their labour have not lost, nor lived nor loved in vain.

XVI.

And it was thus with Adza, she whose song
Made plaintive music but a while ago,
(How short a while it seemed!) when Man was strong,
The yet unquestioned lord of all below.
Now, after forty days of judgment, lo!
Together on this bleak and barren place
They sheltered them in stress of fear and woe,
And each looked blankly in the other's face,
The sole surviving pair of all their impious race.

XVII.

She nestled closer to his side, and said,
"Ithor! my lord and love, were it not well
To make submission now, and bow the head?
How long in safety here we have to dwell,
It needeth sure no prophet to foretell.
Cubit by cubit, still the waters rise,
Still, wave by wave, they roll in longer swell.
Behold them round us level with the skies!
Soon must we part in death—I read it in thine eyes.

XVIII.

"And we have been so happy! Oh! my own!
That happy past, my heart can yet retrace;
I see thee at the feast, about thee thrown
The robe my skill devised thy form to grace.
I see thee rushing god-like in the chase,
Through toil or danger, joyous, proud, and high,
While ever shines a light about thy face,
Caught from the beams of an adoring eye.
My lord, my love, my king! And must I see thee die?

XIX.

"I owe my birth to sires of lordly line!
Mine is the blood of princes, but, behold,
That princely blood can boast a strain divine,
Left by those Sons of Light, of whom 'tis told,
How on the mountains they came down of old,
And pledged to earthly love a heavenly vow,
Their earthly brides in heavenly wings to fold.
Ah! surely these were fairer then than now!
Wilt thou not hear me plead? Nay, never bend thy brow,

XX.

"Nor in displeasure turn away thy face—
The face that day and night I long to greet.
Hast thou not known and proved me of their race
Who grudged no cost their spirit-lords to meet,
And poured their lives out at an angel's feet?
Yet which of these a tale of love could tell
So true as mine? That tale should I repeat?
Hast thou not found, though good or ill befel,
In every turn of fate I loved thee more than well?

XXI.

"Then hear me now! In this last refuge placed,
When of our perished kindred, thou and I,
Two living atoms on the watery waste,
Are left alone, and left, it seems, to die!
Yet not without vague hope of safety nigh,
For, while my weary eyes are strained to gaze
Where meet the misty sea and misty sky,
Unless our grievous plight their senses daze,
Behold, a dim dark shape glides slowly through the haze!

XXII.

" 'Tis surely that strange fabric, long ago
Built in the mountains we shall see no more,
By him, whose wisdom for the time of woe,
A safe and cunning shelter planned, before
The angry skies their floods began to pour.
His aid, our only hope, I bid thee crave.
It cannot shame thee, Ithor, to implore
Man's succour now, thy life and mine to save.
See, love, it lips our feet, the cruel creeping wave."

XXIII.

" It cannot shame me!" he repeated, while
There came a woful lustre in his eye,
Though round his lip was set the changeless smile
Of proud despair, the worst that can defy.
" Is there no shame then, love, when death is nigh,
In fear of death, submission thus to make?
Thus like a frightened child for help to cry?
Would I could find it in my heart to take
The coward's part, and bow my pride for thy dear sake!

XXIV.

"But when I scoffed at him, who, scoffing now,
Rides on in safety, yonder through the gloom,
No foolish boast was mine, no empty vow,
That while on earth it left me standing-room,
Unmoved I would confront this watery doom,
Betray no symptom of remorse nor fear,
My right of Man assert, my rule assume,
While that one spot was left me dry and clear,
And bear me like its lord and king, as I do here!

XXV.

"Yet would I not that thou should'st perish too.
So much thy life is dearer than mine own,
That scarce these rising waters should I rue,
Could I but battle here with death alone!
How dear thou art, too surely hast thou known,
Yet dearer still than thee, I needs must hold
The word I passed, and for that word atone.
What though the boast were somewhat free and bold,
This is no time to flinch, and wish the tale untold.

XXVI.

" But thou art not to suffer thus, because
This stubborn pride of mine can now defy
Our Maker's wrath, as once our Maker's laws.
It needeth but a single suppliant cry
To gain that roomy refuge floating by.
I would not have one precious hair be wet
On that dear head! Then, leave me here to die.
Look to thyself, belovèd one—and yet,
Adza! in time to come thou wilt not quite forget!"

XXVII.

" Forget!" she murmured low, and turned her eyes
On his, and laid her hand within his own.
But that her bosom heaved in fall and rise,
But that each breath came choking through a moan,
She seemed a soulless woman, carved in stone.
Then, roused to sense of all she felt and feared,
She woke, and with her arms about him thrown,
Wept on his breast, till brows and brain were cleared,
And while she wept the Ark passed on and disappeared.

XXVIII.

Not till its outline faded into space,
Cleared from her eyes the cloud of fear and pain;
But now the courage mounted to her face,
And while she raised her head in sweet disdain,
The light of life beamed in her looks again.
For though she was but woman, worn and weak,
Though the devouring waters rose amain,
And though she laid to his a death-cold cheek,
In that fond breast there swelled a love that bade her
    speak.

XXIX.

"And now," she sobbed, exulting, "heart to heart,
Lip glued to lip, together will we drown!
Locked in a last embrace, ere yet we part,
A loving life in loving death to crown,
Cling each to each, and so sink calmly down.
Laugh, cruel waves, your laughter we defy!
Frown, angry heavens, we scorn and mock your frown!
What can we lose or gain, my love and I,
Who hide nor hope to live, nor own a fear to die?

XXX.

"One jot thou hast not 'bated of thy pride,
The pride on which I seem to build mine own,
For I am prouder, shivering by thy side,
Here on our scanty ledge of dripping stone,
Than reigning safe, without thee, on a throne.
Nor would I seek a fairer end than this,
To meet the worst at last with thee alone,
To baffle doom of death in dream of bliss,
And spend my parting breath in one long clinging kiss!"

XXXI.

She spoke—and when she paused, across his brow
There swept a short sharp agony of pain,
That shuddered in his very eyes, for now
Each pulse that beat was sounding on his brain
The knell of hope, that could not live again.
And now the waters coiled about their feet,
To pinion wrestling limbs that strove in vain,
Yet each to other clung. Ah! deadly sweet,
The maddening kiss of lips that nevermore should meet!

XXXII.

Lit by a love, unconquered to the last,
Shone in his eyes a lustre through despair.
And o'er her face a pale sad glory past,
While, of that race rebellious none to spare,
The waters wrapped their shroud about the pair.
Too proud to live, alas! too fair to die.
And thus, their task fulfilled and ended there,
Rose over-head, exulting, fathom-high,
And smiled in calm expanse, unbroken to the sky.

CANTO III.

THE ARK.

I.

YET were not all to perish. On the wave
   A wondrous fabric floated, buoyant still,
   Some remnant of creation that should save,
Ranged and disposed, its goodly bulk to fill;
For He who life bestowed was loth to kill,
And in His wisdom shelter thus prepared
For brutes to stock and human hands to till
   A world renewed, forgiven, cleansed, and spared,
As, ere the evil days, His mercy had declared

II.

When of each beast that trod the solid earth,
When of each bird that clove the yielding air,
Of creeping things produced in slimy birth,
There mounted to the Ark a chosen pair,
Each coupled with its mate, in order fair,
While food of every kind that should supply
Each creature's need was stored and gathered there,
Ruled by a master-hand, a master-eye,
To guide the motley freight that rode 'twixt sea and sky.

III.

None were neglected. Here in slumber lay,
But not beyond that master's ken and care,
Fenced in and well secured, the beast of prey,
To dream it couched in darkling forest lair,
Screened in the leafy brake from noon-day glare,
Or lurked by forest-pools among the trees
Whereto its antlered victim should repair—
Then rose—with quivering nostril snuffed the breeze—
Yawned—stretched its sinewy length, and laid it down at ease.

V.

Here too, majestic in his size and weight,
Propped by a beam, the elephant reclined
With tusks as mightier than his ruthless mate
Like her with lengthened tapering snout designed
In sinuous supple crunch to reach and find
The food he mumbled, calm, sedate and slow—
A beast that seemed informed with human mind
Thus reason more than instinct seemed to show—
More than the brute to feel—more than the man to
    know.

VI.

But he who placed the arresting creature there,
Room for the [...] and the emmet found;
None were too insignificant to spare—
Bird, insect, beast, and reptile of the ground,
All safely folded, each within its bound
Yet each had space to breathe and turn at [...]
Each fed at peace with those that hemmed it round;
And though their ark these creatures seemed to fill
[...] safely dealt us all a passage still

VI.

Because through all their living kingdom, where
The patriarch and his sons passed to and fro,
On great and small they lavished kindly care,
   The nature to observe, the needs to know,
Of all that perched aloft, or stood below;
Whose wistful looks devoured the passing store,
Whose wordless cries arose, their wants to show—
The wolf's long howl, the snort of bristled boar,
The lamb's unquiet bleat, the lordly lion's roar.

VII.

Here, too, were ranged, by keen judicious eyes,
The beasts that went on earth with parted hoof,
But did not chew the cud, or otherwise,—
Clean and unclean, according to the proof,
Each from its converse strictly kept aloof.
While on a timber, laid across above,
'Mong fowls of heaven that roosted in the roof—
A bird of omen next a bird of love,
The muttering raven croaked, and mourned the murmur-
    ing dove.

VIII.

Pining for airy flights in summer skies,
The eagle and the osprey mused apart,
Reposing, but with shining, eager eyes,
And folded pinions, longing to depart
And upward bear the roaming, restless heart,
That yearned for freedom in its waking dream.
And here were birds that wade, and birds that dart
In woven circles, flashing down the stream;
And birds that soar and sing, and birds that sit and scream.

IX.

Crept from its hole the lizard, changing hue
With every change of light the eye to mock.
And burrowing things there were, that shrink from view,
The delving mole, the coney of the rock,
Prolific in its race, its haunts to stock;
And moths and bats, and creatures from the ken
Of morning light to cornered nooks that flock;
And beasts of sloth that, in secluded den,
Sleep out their drowsy lives, unscared by sight of men.

X.

Here lowed the kine; and each with fragrant breath,
And full mild eye, was fain her milk to lend.
Here fawned the dog—true servant to the death
A master's goods to keep, his life defend—
Man's foster-mother, and his firmest friend.
Here fed with stamp and snort the generous steed,
Strength, courage, mettle, glorying to expend,
And through the battle bear his lord at speed,
And strain each gallant limb to serve his utmost need.

XI.

Here, with his sullen head and wreathing crest,
The ungainly camel crouched, morose and strong,
Mistrustful of the heaving board he pressed,
Fierce when aroused to wrath, though suffering long;
Here pondered too the ass, of daily wrong
Forgiving, humble, patient of the rod—
Thereafter, in a burst of praise and song,
Ennobled, while the sacred palms it trod,
And bore, in triumph meek, the Incarnate Son of God.

XII.

But in this goodly Ark, of human lives
Were only these: the builder with his mate,
The three fair sons that helped him, and their wives;
Snatched from the common doom remained but eight,
Content on their Creator's will to wait,
Believing that ere long would cease to lower
The skies, ere long the waters would abate.
Rejoicing in affliction's darkest hour
To lean on endless love, and trust in boundless power.

XIII.

While many a cubit high the flood prevailed,
One hundred days and fifty now were gone,
Nor had those waters yet assuaged nor failed,
And o'er their face the Ark moved slowly on,
As moves on summer lake a gliding swan.
Till widening, strength and lustre while it gained,
Streamed through the mist a sunbeam, pale and wan;
The fountains of the deep at last restrained,
Heaven's windows seemed to close, and now no more it

XIV.

Then, tearing into shreds a filmy veil
Of vapoury wreaths, that floated low and high,
Uprose a breeze, and mounted to a gale,
And drove the clouds careering through the sky—
A mighty wind ere long the earth to dry.
For, faith and hope at last no more to mock,
Drained to the mountain tops the floods drew nigh,
Till, all its timbers quivering in the shock,
Struck the great Ark and poised aground upon a rock.

XV.

Yet still, for forty days, the patriarch chose
In patient pious trust to watch and wait,
Then stretched his hand the window to unclose,
As judging in his wisdom, that of late
Began the waters surely to abate,
And sent a raven forth, to prove and know
If yet there seemed an anchorage for his freight.
Flapped his broad wing the raven, loth to go,
And circled round the Ark, and flitted to and fro.

XVI.

Then did he free a dove, that darted forth,
And up and down she flew, and round and round,
To traverse west and east, and south and north,
And scoured that glassy, watery world, nor found
In all its bright expanse one spot of ground.
Home to the Ark her failing flight she pressed,
And housed her gladly in its sheltering bound,
With dainty feet unsoiled, and spotless breast,
But weak and weary wing, that knew no pause of rest.

XVII.

As holding all creation in his care,
The patriarch waited seven days yet, before
He loosed his scouts again upon the air,
By sea and sky to wander and explore.
The raven went his way, and came no more,
But, by her instinct warned of its decrease,
The dove returned, and in her beak she bore,
In token that the flood should sink and cease,
An olive-branch—the type of hope and love and peace.

XVIII.

Another seven days still he waited, then
A third time freed the bird with gentle hand.
The bird flew swift and noiseless out of ken,
To seek and find a home upon the land,
For, yearning on some growth of green to stand,
To midmost heights of heaven she seemed to soar,
A widening range of upland thence she scanned,
Made for a fringe of woods that lined the shore,
And to the stranded Ark returned she nevermore!

XIX.

Fond, timid, gentle, shrinking like the dove,
That broods and murmurs softly in her nest,
Creeps to man's heart a thing that men call Love,
Surest when hidden, strongest when suppressed,
Of all God's gifts the deadliest or the best—
For at its worst, in needless torture rent,
With self-inflicted pangs it racks the breast,
Or, by its own excesses drained and spent,
It sleeps itself to death—exhausted in content.

XX.

When thus of earthly nature, from the earth,
In earthly greed, its viler food it draws,
But when to heaven it owes a heavenly birth,
Seeks in a loftier sphere its heavenly cause,
And rules its purer growth by heavenly laws;
Then upward to the light it seems to make
Its way, unhindered by mistrust or pause,
And blesses those who give, and those who take,
As each to other yields, each for the other's sake.

XXI.

Thus, when our ark that bird of peace pervades—
Our human ark of joy and hope and fear,
Oh! drive her not away to distant glades!
For dismal is the blank she leaveth here,
—And still the nest is warm, the bird is dear.
Once, twice, she flieth homeward as before,
Forgiveness bearing, our remorse to cheer,
Yet urge her not too often, lest she soar
Far out of human sight, returning nevermore!

XXII.

But now, behold! the patriarch looked around
With careful ken the watery waste to view,
And from the watery waste emerging, found
Another world, bright, beautiful, and new—
Rose peak, and cape, and island, fair of hue,
Fell the great flood, as falls an ebbing tide,
And while the margin sank, the mountain grew,
Its spurs and ridges spreading far and wide.
Thus welcome Land appeared, and stretched on every side.

XXIII.

Soon from their sea-worn refuge, open now,
A long procession filed in order fair;
Teemed with incongruous life the mountain's brow,
Rang with incongruous cries the mountain air,
While all creation, ranging, pair by pair,
In stately measure passed the patriarch's eye:
The patriarch's eye, that scanned with jealous care
Bird, beast, and reptile, moving slowly by,
Creatures that walk, and wade, and bask, and creep, and

XXIV.

Of shapeless stones, uncouth, untouched by tool,
Such as the mountain-fissures could afford,
He took enough and piled them up by rule,
And built therewith an altar to the Lord,
To sacrifice, in thanks for life restored,
Of each clean beast and bird a chosen pair;
Then from the shattered Ark he rent a board,
The mid-most of its crumbling strength that bare,
And set it all aflame to burn his offering there.

XXV.

Yet kindling less than kindly, damp and slow,
To embers charred and smouldering where it lay,
Exuding rather smoke than fire, although
But half-consumed, the patriarch cast away
Its blackened remnant, on a future day
To strike a downward root, and upward tower,
In leafy shelter from the blinding ray
That heats a southern air to furnace-power,
And blisters all the plain in noon's remorseless hour.

XXVI.

Thus tossed and tilted down the steep incline,
Its use fulfilled, a thing of no esteem,
Though once the mystic growth of seed divine,
A torrent, plunging headlong, caught the beam,
And whirled it, like a leaf, upon its stream,
And leaped and laughed, to snatch it from the hill;
Then bore it statelier on, as it would seem,
Triumphant such a waif to float, until
Constrained to yield it up, God's purpose to fulfil.

XXVII.

When shrunk and ebbing from its swollen pride,
By rush of mountain floods no longer fed,
On distant verge, that marked its fallen tide,
Far from the silver track that formed its bed,
Where wound the dwindling river like a thread,
Its burden it should leave aground and dry,
From rich alluvial soil to shoot and spread
In growth gigantic, rearing to the sky
A leafy crest and arms that tossed and waved on high.

XXVIII.

But now in rolling wreaths of smoke, to spend
Its goodly fragrance on the freshened air,
Began the patriarch's offering to ascend,
While rose to reach his God the patriarch's prayer.
Reverend he stood, with feet in homage bare,
Direct from their Creator, over all
His creatures to receive dominion there,
That every moving thing should be his thrall,
To quail beneath his eye, and tremble at his call.

XXIX.

Thus for the brute creation to obey
The rule of Man, subservient to his might,
Beasts of the field at need to fell and slay,
And use them like the herbs, he gave him right.
But warned him in the fratricidal fight,
If ruthless hands were stained with guilty red,
How life for life such trespass must requite,
In just reprisals on the murderer's head:
" Who sheddeth blood of Man, Man's law his blood shall

XXX.

For Man in image of Himself, God made;
And with a father's condescending care,
To Man's finite conception thus conveyed
A sense of Him, to whom he cried in prayer.
Nay, in that likeness all our sins to bear,
And ransom with His blood our erring race,
Man's shape corporeal He vouchsafed to wear.
Who then shall dare that image to deface,
Doth outrage to his God, of whom it beareth trace.

XXXI.

Also He gave him pledge, so long as rolled
Our earthly ages in their courses here,
That summer's heat should wait on winter's cold,
That harvest after seed-time should appear,
To mark the changes of each passing year.
And thus assured him hope, without alloy,
Of labouring daily on, unvexed by fear,
To eat the fruits of toil, in thankful joy
That this, his world, a flood should never more destroy.

XXXII.

The token of that promise, firm and true,
For coming time established, then to show,
Sun-striped, in bands of each prismatic hue,
Behold! against the cloud he set his bow,
That henceforth man should never fail to know
How bright a smile could shine behind their frown,
And span the skies with glory of its glow—
An arch to compass heaven—a radiant crown—
A bridge for angel feet to travel up and down.

XXXIII.

And thus, the voice of instinct to obey,
When from the Ark had trooped an endless train
Of creatures, cooped therein for many a day,
With life and strength renewed, of freedom fain,
(For none seemed willing to return again,)
With those stout sons, his mission to fulfil,
The patriarch, too, went down into the plain
The vine to plant, the soil to cleanse and till,
And people many a land, urged by his Maker's will.

XXXIV.

For all above was bright and joyous now,
And all below was balmy, warm, and dry;
Splintered the sunshine on the mountain's brow,
Hushed in its heat the valleys seemed to lie,
Nor moved the cloud that floated on the sky.
Great sheets of wild flowers painted plains untrod:
Luxuriant bursts of Nature, low and high,
Wove wreaths of verdure o'er a teeming sod,
And fertile earth, forgiven, looked smiling up to God.

BOOK III.

THE TREE.

BOOK III

THE TRIBE

BOOK III.

THE TREE.

IN midmost heaven the sun was high,
Stirred not a breath to cool the sky,
   And fell, like fiery rain,
Sheets of a bright and blinding glare
That seemed to scorch the upper air,
   And, pouring down amain,
Bathed in a burning glow of gold,
Rock, mountain, valley, wood and wold.
Scarce could the ox his head uphold,
   Of stream and shelter fain;

Scarce could the lamb find strength to bleat,
So fierce and hard the sun-beam beat,
The pasture shrivelled at its feet;
And glimmered through a blaze of heat
  The Cities of the Plain.
Pleasant and goodly to the eye,
With lordly tower and palace high,
And circling rampart crowned.
In every level space and bare,
By temple, terrace, street and square,
The gracious palm was feathering there,
And gushed the fountain, free and fair,
To slake the stones and cool the air.
And spice, and myrrh, and odours rare,
And raiment rich, and costly ware,
And all that wealth for ease could spare
  Were freely scattered round.
While, wasteful in his pomp and pride,
Feasted the rich, and at his side
The starving beggar moaned and died,
  Unsheltered on the ground.

Revelled the strong in wine and lust,
The weak were trampled in the dust;
None were remorseful, none were just,
   And none were righteous found.
Though brave and bright those buildings gleamed
But whited sepulchres they seemed,
   Corrupt and rank within,
And all without a mocking show,
A bitter strife of high and low—
Oppression, treachery, wrath and woe,
A downward stream in endless flow
   Of selfishness and sin.
By heaven and earth alike accursed,
Cities, the vilest and the worst,
In every thought of evil nursed,
In deeds of darkness ever first
   Each outrage to begin.
So bold in error man had grown,
Guilt, that no penance could atone,
His wicked heart rejoiced to own,
   And dragged him through the mire,

> Exulting in its loathsome stain,
> Each hideous vice to entertain,
> From no pollution to refrain
> In foulest of desire.

Nor praise he offered to his Lord, nor prayer,
Nor pity for his brother felt, nor care,—
His only thought, with every passing hour,
To feed his fancy, or increase his power.
Prompted by lust of heart and sense and eye,
With boldest sinners in their sins to vie;
From dark excesses drawing mad delight,
And breaking Nature's law by day and night.
With lies and slander nourished, clothed in guile,
Presumptuous, yet disturbed with dread the while—
Sleek, pampered coward, vilest of the vile!

> And Woman, from her nobler self debased,

Now for a whim exalted, now disgraced,
Each purer, holier feeling to destroy,
In turn a dupe, an idol, and a toy,
With shameless haste descending from the throne
That, while she queened it there, was hers alone,

Unsexed, undone, to gain a worthless end,
Her lures, her love, her beauty stooped to lend.
No more inciting to heroic deed,
The hero she was proud of, proud to lead,
His hopes her own, his triumph her reward,
Merged wholly in the nature she adored—
No more in mutual cares of wedded state,
Friend, monitress, and counsellor of her mate,
Urgent to claim a wife's unchallenged part,
The undivided empire of a heart—
But like the robe, that in her dainty pride,
For lightest speck or stain she flung aside—
A gaudy thing to covet, and to prize—
An empty thing—to leave and to despise—
Her lawful rights compelled to extort or crave,
Alternately a tyrant and a slave.
Yet was she fair, in spite of every wile:
The painted blush, the false and artful smile,
The known device, the too alluring bait,
The lisping accent, and the mincing gait.

For still, though foul and fallen, there lurked a trace
Of angel-beauty in her woman's face,
To show, through haggard eyes and altered mien,
Not what she was, but what she might have been;
Nor seemed she wholly lost, for at her worst,
Some soft and gentle fancies still she nursed,
Hid in her inmost heart and kept it fast
Some sweet remembrance of a happier past;
Still, by her subtle woman's instinct taught,
Preserved, through guilt and shame, some purer thought,
Fed in maternal cares a holier fire,
And loved the babe, though weary of the sire.
But, like a spreading ulcer, festering sore,
That wastes the flesh, and eats into the core,
Throughout the frame-work of the social plan
A foul corrupting taint of evil ran—
A taint that seemed imparted in a breath,
Unerring symptom of a moral death,
Pervading and infecting high and low,
Fore-runner of impending wrath and woe.

For this, the wanton rich in scarlet state
Swelled high with pride, and scorned his neighbour's hate;
For this the weary poor, oppressed and ground,
In broodings of revenge his comfort found.
For hearts of common interest thus bereft,
Nor faith, nor truth, nor honour, could be left.
Intrigued the feeble, tyrannized the strong,
And each to all the rest did foul and shameful wrong.
 Yet one there was whose spirit grieved
  Such hideous sinks of vice to know,
 One who in God and man believed,
 And hope of pardon thus conceived
 For sinners at their worst, reprieved,
  In very doom of instant woe.
 One who in youth had never failed
  To serve his Lord with praise and prayer,
 Whose pious plea had oft availed,
 And oft on Mercy's ear prevailed,
  His erring fellow-men to spare.

For still in sacred rite, and holy test,
The son of Terah godliest seemed, and best.
Therefore his Lord preserved him as he went,
By flood and field, in city, cave, and tent;
Coerced the royal Egyptian to forbear
From fraud or force, though Sarah's face was fair;
And led him out of Pharaoh's treacherous land,
As leads a sire his youngest by the hand,
Increased his substance, gave him store untold
Of camels, asses, flocks and herds, and gold.
Far as his sight could travel, bade him know,
On him and his the earth he would bestow,
And brought him, rest and shelter to obtain,
Where towered the tree, by Mamre on the plain,
Predestined from his wanderings there to cease,
And taste a holy calm in sweet repose and
    peace.
    For ages now had past,
    Since on its margin cast,
A sinking river left the mystic beam

From a shattered ark up-torn,
By a torrent hither borne
And stranded, when it dwindled to a stream,
To strike its downward root,
And push its upward shoot,
And wave its spreading branches free and fair,
Like some darkling forest glade,
A mass of rippling shade
To shelter all the creatures of the air.
No goodlier it grew,
When Noah came to hew
Its substance, for completion of his plan;
Nor threw its shadow round,
On wider space of ground,
In early age of patriarchal man.
And he who sat beneath it there,
With solemn looks and reverent air,
No whit less worthy showed
Than Lamech, Jared, Cainan, Seth,
Or Enoch, who, absolved from death,

With God in heaven abode.
For though his strength was waning now,
　　Though front and temples bare,
And lines of thought that scored his brow
　　Showed sign of time and care;
Though beard and locks were snowy white,
Shone in his glance the steady light
Of godly courage, true and bright,
That battles calmly for the right,
Nor doubts to conquer all in fight,
Armed with the undefeated might
　　Of sacrifice and prayer.
Grave was his aspect, clear his eye,
Serene and open like the sky,
Ample his frame, and towering high.
　　While free and firm he trod,
With kingly gait of conscious worth,
As one deputed here on earth,
In time of danger or of dearth,
　　A viceroy, by his God.

His tent was pitched upon the plain
    Of Mamre, near the sacred tree;
For there behoved him to remain,
His angel-guests to entertain,
    That thus the patriarch might foresee
The noble future of his line,
Predestined by the will divine,
In furtherance of its great design,
    A chosen race to be.
A chosen race, preserved to stand
Before their Lord in many a land,
Protected by his favouring hand.
In number like the grains of sand,
    Uncounted, by the sea.
Screened by those branches from the burning ray,
He sat before his tent at noon of day,
And looking outward o'er the plain, espied
Three coming travellers faring side by side;
In haste he rose and ran to meet them there,
And bowed him to the ground, and spoke them fair,

And prayed them turn aside to do him grace,
Abiding in the shade some little space,
Their limbs to rest, and wash their dusty feet,
And cheer their weary hearts with bread to eat.

Fresh from the herd, the tenderest calf he slew,
Hot from the hearth the daintiest cake he drew;
A courteous greeting gave each honoured guest,
And bade him freely welcome to the best.
The simple meal before them thus he set,
And stood at hand to serve them while they ate.
Then spoke the men of Sarah as she went,
In household cares assiduous, through the tent,
Yet woman-like, desirous still to know
Their converse, while she flitted to and fro;
Thus did she hear their promise to her lord,
That now, though youth was passed, she should afford
An heir for long continuance of his race
In many a good and noble name to trace,

Through prophet, priest, and king, the holy line,
And culminate at last in One divine!
Sprung from *her* babe, hereafter to be born.
And while she listened, low she laughed in scorn.
"Who laughed within?" the stranger said. "Not I!"
Answered the woman, eager to deny,
Nor trusting yet the power of Him, whose word,
By angel-lips declared, she overheard.
For these, so fair of aspect, so serene
In dignity of bearing and of mien,
In looks so gracious, yet so calm and high,
Were surely God's own angels from the sky,
And in their eyes a holy lustre shone,
Reflected from the great eternal throne.
Their presence, goodlier than of mortal men,
Yet not devoid of awe to mortal ken,
Though clothed in shape corporeal, made them seem
To mortal sense like visions in a dream.
Even as they spoke, the patriarch's spirit stirred
With reverend joy, accepting every word,

The hopeful tidings hopefully received;
And while the woman sneered, the man believed
Not long they tarried: ere the sun was low,
Though pleaded hard the host, they rose to go;
Bound for the godless cities of the plain,
Through scorching heat to journey forth again,
They turned their faces from that godly tent,
But left behind a blessing as they went.
So to our hearts, with cares of life oppressed,
There cometh now and then the heavenly guest,
An unexpected stranger, hither brought,
In guise of kindly deed, or holy thought,
Or pitying love, a brother's woe that bears,
And thus bestowing help and tears and prayers,
We entertain an angel unawares.
Not here he makes his home, nor deigns to stay,
His task fulfilled, too soon he speeds away,
To leave us blankly gazing where he shone,
For lo! the tent is void, the guest is gone!

Yet still a holy light pervades the place
Where late he stood, and eyed us face to face.
Still of his words, that blessed us as they fell,
Caught in our hearts, an echo seems to dwell.
And here, where even now his footstep trod,
We know we held communion with our God.
Nor righteous tents alone their shelter lend,
When strangers such as these from heaven descend;
By many a rough and weary path they roam,
In many a wayward heart they find a home,
O'er many a gloomy nook the lustre shed,
That leaves a ray reflected when 'tis fled.
And many a humbled, saddened soul they cheer,
That longs to aim at heaven, though grovelling here,
Like some poor bird with broken wing that lies,
To cower and pant, and upward at the skies
Direct a pleading gaze, with sad and suffering eyes.
Gaze on, and upward still, poor wounded bird,
Though dumb thy plea, believe it shall be heard.

Soiled, stricken, helpless, hopeless, only trust!
A tender hand shall take thee from the dust,
The ruffled plumes shall smooth with careful love,
And lift thee gently to thy home above.
Nor deem too lowly, or too vile thou art,
For there the lowliest, vilest, have a part:
The good, the bad, the early, and the late,
Who kneel and knock, find entrance at the gate.
The last are pardoned freely as the first,
And He who suffers long hath welcome for the worst.

    Brief was the hour of respite lent,
    The strangers turned them from the tent,
        And journeyed forth again.
    With slow, unwilling steps they went,
    As though while Mercy might relent,
    Affording leisure to repent,
        Ere fell the flaming rain—
    The floods of fire by vengeance sent,
    When time of grace was past and spent,
    To seethe and scorch in their descent
        The Cities of the Plain.

Attending on their footsteps, there,
   A holy instinct to obey,
With pious zeal, and reverend care,
   The patriarch brought them on their way.
And side by side while thus they walked,
   Unfolding the Almighty plan,
It seemed that when the angel talked,
   The voice of God conversed with man,
And told the doom was hovering nigh.
For, vengeance to provoke on high,
   From Sodom and Gomorrha came
A daily challenge to the sky,
Uprising in its ceaseless cry
   Of grievous sin and shame!
And, therefore, Mercy, suffering long,
   But willing yet to spare,
Came down from heaven to sift the throng,
And seek amongst the fierce and strong,
If any from rebellious wrong
   Had wisdom to forbear,

Before the day of pardon should expire,
And holy vengeance fall in streams of fire.

    Passed from the patriarch's sight,
    Like phantoms of the night,
His angel-guests, yet gazed he where they trod,
    And stood in rapture, there
    To wrestle hard in prayer,
While pleading for the sinners with his God.
    That if within the bound
    Of their city might be found
A tale of fifty righteous men and true,
    For the righteous fifty's sake
    No vengeance would He take,
But have mercy on the many for the few.
    Then promised him the Lord,
    If Sodom could afford
But fifty such within the city wall,
    For the fifty that were there,
    All the others would He spare,

And the record of His justice would recall.
    But the patriarch, not in vain,
    Made petition yet again,
That if five of these were lacking from the tale,
    For the forty and the five
    He would save the whole alive,
In His mercy that was never known to fail.
    And abated more and more,
    Till at last, if half-a-score
Of the righteous had been found to stand the test,
    Though of good and honest men
    Could be numbered only ten,
There was promise of a pardon for the rest.

Thus having stood before his Maker's face,
Returned the pious patriarch to his place;
And while he pondered on the words of awe,
His soul deplored the doom his sense foresaw.
In pity for the madness of his kind,
And wonder man could be so false and blind;

Man, who had brain to reason, yet withstood,
In dogged mood perverse, the obvious good,
Sunk in the very indolence of sin,
Because the obvious evil hemmed him in;
Because of knaves a few, of fools a throng,
Confounding every phase of right and wrong,
Excused a common guilt, a common shame,
By pleading all the others did the same.
How strange it seemed laborious lives to spend
In eager aims at some illusive end;
To chase the phantoms born of foolish thought,
That proved but empty shadows, lost when caught;
To pass their days in toil, their nights in dread,
And waste their strength for that which was not bread;
The poisoned cup with thirsty lip to meet,
And find its deadly draught not even sweet;
Hope, health, and heaven to lose beyond recall,
Nor gain a glimpse of pleasure after all!
How sad to think that every sinner there
Was born the rich inheritance to share,

That, like a child in wanton, wayward play,
Of wild misguided mood, he flung away!
How sad to know that each immortal soul
Turned with a purpose from the heavenly goal,
And wandered on with wavering steps to find
The sure destruction of the wilful blind.
As when a madman's hand the kerchief ties,
With cunning smile of madness, round his eyes,
And thus where yawns a dizzy void, below
Some ledge of cliff, he saunters to and fro,
Till straying o'er the verge abrupt and bare,
His stumbling footstep meets the empty air,
Roused by the plunge that curdles every vein,
One flash of reason clears his startled brain,
And waking to his folly and his fate,
He tears the bandage down, enlightened all too late!
Such troubled thoughts the patriarch's soul oppressed,
Disturbed his dreams, and vexed him from his rest,
Pursued him through the watches of the night,
And drove him from his tent with morning-light;

Help to his kind though eager to afford,
Yet, jealous for the honour of his Lord,
To mark the fierce excess of human guile
Aroused his wrath, but grieved his heart the while.
Foreboding thus some hideous sight to see,
He stood at dawn beneath the mystic tree,
And sorrowing for the doom so close at hand,
Looked forth in sadness on the guilty land.

    Behold! the day of wrath and woe
        Had risen with the sun!
    For rolling upward, thick and slow,
    In heavy volume from below,
    Lit by a red and angry glow,
        To lurid hues of dun,
The smoke was pouring forth amain,
Where seethed the surface of the plain,
Where floods of fire had fallen like rain,
Where now repentance was in vain,
        And judgment had begun.
The shapes of death that veiling cloud
Wrapped in its folds, as in a shroud,

No tongue of man can tell—
The anguish, too intense to bear,
The wild appeal, the fierce despair,
The quivering forms that in the glare,
With shriek and shout, and tossing hair,
Writhed, leaped, and flitted here and there,
 Like tortured souls in hell.
One had been clad in purple vest,
 And feasted on a throne;
In rags and filth had one been drest,
 And mumbled at a bone.
But he who sat in royal array,
 To drain a cup of gold,
And he, who naked by the way,
A scarred and loathsome leper lay,
To beg the crust from day to day,
 That scarce could life uphold,
Were equal now in equal plight.
In panic of a blind affright,
In agonies that longed for flight

With impotent desire.
The beggar's morsel shrivelled up,
On lordly lips the golden cup
　Was turned to molten fire.
Man, beast, and building, as it past,
Curled in the flame, and withered fast,
Like cinders from a furnace cast,
Consumed in the consuming blast
　Of God's avenging ire.
Lo! blistering in his harness here,
The man of war, aghast with fear,
Clutched in a shaking hand the spear,
　Or half unsheathed the sword;
And cursed the arm that thus could fail,
And cursed the torture of his mail,
The glowing steel of no avail
　Resistance to afford!
And there the harlot cowered to hide
The dainty face, that in her pride
To God and man had leered and lied,

So false and yet so fair!
The dainty face with shameless brow,
In dust and ashes sprinkled now,
That muttered many a senseless vow,
  And many a soulless prayer.
Yet when the fire-blast smote her sore,
The covering from her neck she tore,
And in it wrapped the babe she bore
  To shelter it from harm.
She lived, degraded and defiled,
She died, with pain and terror wild,
A sinner with a sinless child
  Encircled in her arm;
And when their souls to judgment flew,
Mayhap the purer of the two
Its scared and shrinking comrade drew,
  The Pardoner to meet.
Mayhap, in that atoning day,
The Mother's love had wiped away
The woman's guilt, whose spirit lay
  Forgiven at His feet!

Again looked forth the patriarch, and again ;
Still was the smoke ascending from the plain,
Though quenched the fire, and hushed the roaring blast,
For now God's purpose was fulfilled at last.
While, like a pall by mourners' hands outspread,
Floated that sable curtain o'er the Dead.
With all his heart the son of Terah grieved,
Yet steadfastly, with all his soul, believed
The God he worshipped righteous was, and just,
And though his Lord should slay, the man could trust.
When therefore the appointed time was spent,
He trooped his flocks and herds, and struck his tent
To journey southward, by Divine command,
And find in other climes a fairer land,
His footsteps turning from the sacred tree,
That stood in all its goodly growth, to be
A token of the Almighty's mercy still,
The witness of his truth, and record of His will.

BOOK IV.

THE BEAM.

BOOK IV.

THE BEAM

PART I.

SCHAMIR.

A MURMUR on the mountain side,
   A moaning in the breeze,
   A voice where passing shadows glide
Amongst the forest-trees.
A stir of leaves along the brake,
   A rustle in the glade,
A ripple moving o'er the lake,
   A whisper through the shade.
By wood and wold, by sea and sky,
The rush of wings, where spirits fly,

Of man's untutored ear and eye
    Unheeded and unknown;
For these, though lost to mortal ken,
Can yet control the fate of men,
And trouble all their future, when
    It seemeth most their own.
In every human life below,
These are the powers that surely know
The measure of its weal and woe,
    The sentence of its doom;
And whether leading it astray,
Or guiding it along the way,
That, step by step, and day by day,
    Attend it to the tomb;
And these the powers at whose desire
    The elements are still,
For earth and water, air and fire,
    Are subject to their will,
By His decree, who gave them right,
In tasks proportioned to their might,

As lower than the sons of light,
    Such purpose to fulfil.
Perverse they are, and boast to trace
Descent from the rebellious race,
    As stubborn in their sphere,
Wild, wayward, rather fierce than bold,
Skilled to elude the captor's hold,
And in their cunning, best controlled
    By mastery of fear.
They tumble in the ferns at night,
    They dance behind the tree,
They gambol in the fading light,
They ride the moon-beam, silver-bright,
    Aslant upon the sea.
Their revels in the moss they keep
    Around the crystal spring;
Beneath her leaves they peer and peep,
And when the lily nods to sleep,
About her bending neck they leap,
    And clasp her while they swing.

Wherever wealth of nature teems,
Where in her daintiest dress she seems
More beautiful than morning dreams,
By river, rock, and dell,
By flowery paths, and pleasant ways,
By tangled copse, and leafy maze,
Asleep in summer's golden haze,
  These spirits love to dwell.
But yet, apart from mortal eye,
The rule of man they still defy,
Unless he wrests it from on high,
  In store of knowledge strong.
And when perforce they bow before
Resistless might of human lore,
It seems to scourge and vex them sore,
  As galled with grievous wrong.
Like prisoned birds their wings that beat
  Against the prison-bars,
Now here, now there, they turn and meet,
In countless rings their flights repeat,

And deem their freedom incomplete
  Amidst the very stars,
Because the summons has gone forth,
And east and west, and south and north,
  That summons when they hear,
Though stands the mighty word alone,
A word engraven on a stone,
To mortal lips as yet unknown,
  Unheard by mortal ear;
When through the depths of space it rings,
With cowering and submissive wings
  The spirits, far and near,
From all the realms wherein they dwell,
The border lands of heaven and hell,
Before his face, who spoke the spell,
  Must hasten to appear!
Nor one so wayward nor so bold,
  As that command to disobey,
Which bade him to the throne of gold,
  Where sat his lord in royal array—

A king who reigned o'er many a land,
    Whom other kings must bow before,
Whose gold was countless as the sand,
    Whose rule was boundless as the shore—
A king on whose behalf were met
    The choicest gifts from Heaven that fall,
Wealth, glory, power, success, and yet
    Whose wisdom far exceeded all
In knowledge, that had found a key
    To every hoard of human lore,
To secrets of the earth and sea,
    The sun, the sky, the stars, and more,
To magic power of sign and spell,
That viewless beings could compel,
From viewless haunts wherein they dwell,
    To do his bidding here.
By toil or distance undeterred,
In virtue of the awful word
That all their subtler nature stirred
    To agony of fear.

With eyes abashed, and drooping wing,
Each spirit as it passed the King
Did homage to the mystic ring
   That held it thus in thrall.
And he who on his finger wore
The gem such potent charm that bore,
With calm regard that vexed them sore
   Looked steadfastly on all,
Till, parting from the spirit band,
With but a gesture of his hand,
One shadowy form, he bade it stand.
   Selected from the rest;
And though it seemed to quail with fear,
It could not choose but venture near,
And mark with an attentive ear
   The Wizard-king's behest.
'Twas but a phantom, dim and gray,
In darkling forest-nooks that lay,
And loved to watch the stream at play,
   And with it dance along,

To catch the sunbeam as it strayed,
To chase the echo through the glade,
Or, lurking in the leafy shade,
    To mock the wild-birds' song.
And every creature's haunt it knew,
And flowers of every scent and hue,
And weeds and herbs, and plants that grew
    In every lonely place.
But still it shrunk from human sight,
At human call it took to flight,
And most in hatred and despite
    It held the human face.
Thus drawing near the throne,
Unwillingly compelled,
It dared not writhe nor utter moan,
    Though all its pride rebelled
Subjection by a mortal hand to own,
And hear its master speak in calm imperious tone.
" Because o'er forest things I gave thee power,
I send thee back thy forest haunts to scour,

Forbidding thee by glade or lawn to stray,
Or cease thine urgent quest from day to day,
Until thou find and lay before my throne
A substance that can cut the hardest stone.
Nor tempered steel, nor iron shall it be,
From such polluting contact must be free
The virgin blocks that I have sought and stored
To build me up the Temple of the Lord.
Yet, tempered steel and iron to surpass
Must cut as cuts a diamond into glass,
With smooth and easy action gliding through
The rock that steel and iron may not hew.
That such a force existeth in the waste
Well do I know, and therefore bid thee haste
To seek it far and wide through thy domain,
Nor hope forgiveness if thy search be vain,
Nor dare return until thy task be done.
Behold! thy Lord hath spoken—now begone!"
  Obedient to the stern discharge
  Accorded by the imperious King,

Rejoiced to be again at large,
The Spirit flew on ready wing;
Coerced by that resistless spell,
To search in dingle and in dell,
Through all the haunts it loved so well,
    From rise to set of sun.
And many a mountain, spent and sore,
And many a valley traversed o'er,
And many a cast it made, before
    The weary chase was done.
Till, ranging by the water-side,
A low and lonely nook it spied,
Wherein the moor-hen thought to hide
    The young ones of her nest.
Relieved at last, it flitted round
That secret spot, and marked the ground,
As deeming it had surely found
    The object of its quest.
Then, taking counsel of its craft,
    It brought a slab of granite bare

And laid it on the hole, and laughed,
   And waited—watching there.
When back the moor-hen came at length
   To find her portals barred,
She smote with all her tiny strength
   That surface smooth and hard;
Then to the wilderness once more
   She fled, for help to seek,
And swift returning, lo! she bore
   A something in her beak,
A little worm her need to aid,
   A creature on the granite laid,
That soon an easy way had made,
   And bored it through and through,
But, ere the task she set about,
   The Spirit with a sudden shout
So scared her that she dropped it out,
   And thus away she flew!
Pleased was that cruel, cunning elf,
And laughed again within itself.

>As laughs the pyat o'er its pelf,
>> So rich a prize to own.
>> And sped rejoicing on the way,
>> Its dreaded master to obey,
>> Exulting such a gift to lay
>> Before the golden throne.

Behold! at last the monarch's purpose gained,
The instrument his wisdom sought obtained.
Soon in its pride uprose the sacred shrine
By human glory reared to power divine.
Block laid on block, the weighty work was piled,
By kiss of earthly metal undefiled,
For edge of earthly metal might not hew
The masses whence that stately Temple grew.
Thus, towering daily in the people's eyes,
Men looked and marvelled at its goodly size,
And deemed it strange such mason work should stand,
So deftly fitted by the mason's hand,
Each corner so exactly squared by rule,
Yet still unheard the ring of mason's tool;

The chisel and the graving-point unknown,
And all untouched by steel the virgin stone.
None knew the magic force their King had brought
To bear on labour by the power of Thought;
Nor deemed that through the granite day and night
A little worm was boring out of sight,
The task-work to fulfil of him who bade
That little worm, called Schamir, to his aid.
To whom of all the human race alone
The creature's mystic properties were known,
Who in the volumes of a wizard's lore
Had learned its uses, and the name it bore;
Whose wisdom from the desert could compel
A thousand such, by stress of sign and spell;
Who, planning work too hard for human hand,
Held each resource of nature at command,
And found a band of slaves the toil to ply,
In all the powers of earth and sea and sky.
From dawn of morning thus, to evening's close,
The people marvelled as the Temple rose,

And held their breath, and stopped upon the way
To mark its noiseless growth from day to day,
And wagged their beards, and racked their brains in vain,
And asked their solemn elders to explain.
Answered the elders, solemn and sedate,
"Behold! The King is wise, and God is great!"
But where, though sought beyond the farthest bound
That girds the King's dominion, can be found
A beam so huge, and yet so tough of grain,
As shall the Temple's weighty roof sustain?
Behold! where still an ancient tree remains,
The goodliest growth of all the Southern plains,
A faithful record of the past, though dumb,
And truthful prophet of the time to come.
Nor in its bulk diminished, nor decayed,
Since o'er the patriarch's tent it threw a shade.
When earthly paths the heavenly footstep trod,
And holy father Abraham spake with God.
That ancient tree must fall by royal award,
An offering to the glory of the Lord,

While o'er its trunk the woodman's axe must gleam,
And carve from out its bulky heart a beam
To prop the noblest building man could raise,
The house of prayer, and sacrifice, and praise.
Two goodly columns, towering in their pride,
Uprose to flank the porch on either side—
Fit portals for the gate of God's abode,
And holy names on each the King bestowed
In words of mystery and fear, that meant
The " Guidance " and the " Strength " on which he leant
In memory of that early penance placed,
When weary Israel wandered through the waste,
And looked for God's own sign to lead them right—
Pillar of cloud by day, of fire by night.
Connecting each with each, the beam was laid,
And those who came to worship, or to trade,
O'erhanging thus, looked down on many a race,
From many a land, that thronged the sacred place.
For all the earth had learned the monarch's name,
And all the earth was greedy of his fame.

Kings, princes, sages, gathered far and near,
His wealth to covet, and his words to hear.
To mark his wisdom, marvelled e'en the wise,
And fools beheld his riches with surprise.
But wise and fools alike were fain to own,
That when they bowed before the golden throne
A-blaze with flash of gems on every side,
And thus beheld the lustre of its pride,
For once the voice of Rumour had not lied,
And he who sat thereon in matchless state,
Was justly called the Rich the Wise, the Great!

THE BEAM.

PART II.

THE QUEEN OF THE SOUTH.

FAR in a southern land,
    Beneath unclouded skies,
    Where shoots the palm from tawny sand,
To shade the camels as they stand
    Athirst, with sullen eyes,
Descending from his drooping beast,
Behold! a merchant of the East,
    Who many a clime had seen,
Whose wares in many a mart were sought,
Who many a bale had sold and bought,
And many a costly present brought
    In tribute to the Queen.

For all who travelled far and near,
Before her throne she bade appear,
Their journeyings and escapes to hear.

And wondrous tales they told:
Of jewelled plains where posies grew,
In gems of every shade and hue;
Where diamonds lay, like drops of dew,

And rivers ran with gold;
Of monstrous birds with scarlet crest
And silver wings, and ivory breast,
That brooded in a monstrous nest,

O'er pearls of monstrous size;
Of gardens girt with magic wall,
Lest priceless fruits should outward fall,
And dragons watching over all,

With fierce and flaming eyes;
Of mountain path and forest glade,
Where every winding turn betrayed,
At every step the traveller made,
Through gleam and gloom of light and shade.

Some new and strange surprise.
But none who thus discharged their freight
Of marvels at the palace gate,
Such tales of wonder could narrate,
As he who had beheld of late
    The greatest King on earth.
Had marked o'er all the Eastern land,
His sceptre swayed by God's command,
His righteous rule, his reaching hand,
His riches countless as the sand,
    His wisdom and his worth.
And thus returning homeward, fain
The Southern Queen to entertain
With glories of that monarch's reign,
    He bowed him reverend down,
And kneeling, from his lowly place,
To pray her of her queenly grace
For leave to speak a little space,
Looked upward in the loveliest face
    That ever wore a crown.

Swarthy she was, but comely in the glows
That flushed her crimson, like a damask rose,
With coil of jetty locks a gleam that shed.
Like shining serpents twisted round her head,
And arching brows, and tawny cheek, but clear,
Straight as a palm, and graceful as a deer.
While in her eyes there shone the tender light
We see reflected in a summer's night,
The token of a richer, warmer ray,
A lustre that shall come with coming day—
Eyes that had never languished, longed, nor wept,
For, all untouched, one half her being slept—
Soft, pleading, shy, unwilling to declare
The hidden spark that surely smouldered there;
Yet waited only till the moment came,
When answering eyes should rouse the answering flame,
And soul and sense and instinct should conspire
To kindle all her nature into fire.
With pliant limbs, and shape beyond compare,
She moved like flowing water, smooth and fair,

. . ..

In every step and gesture showed the trace
Of desert freedom, curbed to courtly grace.
But that her lot forbade in tents to dwell,
Had laughed the loveliest damsel at the well,
For beauty crowned her matchless brows, before
The jewelled crown of royalty she wore,
And in her every turn of mood and mien
She bloomed a Woman, while she walked a Queen.
Thus in a woman's keen desire to learn
All that her home, herself, can least concern,
Or by a woman's instinct urged to run
Direct on danger it were wise to shun,
That travelled merchant now she drew aside,
And with unceasing questions shrewdly plied,
While he, encouraged by the Royal command,
Detailed the wonders of the Eastern land;
Its monarch's glories prompted to relate,
Dwelt on his power, his riches, and his state.
But most of all the Southern Queen inclined
To know the workings of that master-mind,

Entranced, as though, even here, she heard and hung
On every accent of the golden tongue;
And in the casket of her memory stored
The precepts from that fount of wisdom poured;
Nor drooped her eye, nor did her patience fail,
While thus the Eastern merchant told his tale:

"My Queen, there lies a pleasant land
    For those who lead their camels forth
To journey o'er the waste of sand
    That bounds us on the east and north.
A land where in a fruitful soil
    The olive and the fig-tree grow—
A land of corn, and wine, and oil,
    A land where milk and honey flow;
Where every man enjoys his own,
    Nor holds his right by bow and spear—
As safe, unguarded, and alone,
    As one begirt with warriors here.
For there the strong and mastering hand
    Is guided by the wise decree,

And while his law protects the land,
    The King declares his people free,
And not with freedom only blessed,
    For stated feasts their labours cheer,
And though the toil be easy, lest
    The husbandman should seem oppressed,
One day in every seven they rest,
    And all the seventh year.
Yet none so poor and naked go,
    But meat and clothes they can bestow
According to their state;
    And, while the righteous work to speed,
They help a brother at his need,
    The hungry mouths they gladly feed
Of strangers at the gate.
    A steadfast purpose, not in vain,
They ever seem to entertain
    In wealth and ease to live;
With busy craft of hand and brain
    They toil their object to attain,

And if they dearly love to gain
  They better love to give.
Thus while their bounty more and more
  Increases with increasing store,
Though keen they are and wise,
  So high their trading profits mount,
Silver they deem of no account,
  And gold they scarcely prize.
For ships by hundreds, and by scores,
  To furl their sails on foreign shores
From every port the nation pours,
  With daring seamen manned;
And thus all curious things and fair,
  Myrrh, spices, gems, and costly ware,
Apes, ivory, peacocks, strange and rare,
  Are brought from every land.
And where to grace the dazzling throne,
That flames with every precious stone,
The glorious monarch sits alone
  In kingly state, behold!

To keep the steps, a guardian band,
By six and six on either hand,
In living likeness deftly planned,
And large as life, twelve lions stand,
   Of pure and solid gold!
But all these pomps of outward pride,
   And gauds of empty show,
Are but as autumn leaves that hide
   The goodly fruit below;
For, used by great ones of the earth,
Such matters seem of little worth,
   Scarce noticed or required.
And that wise King himself hath told,
Though neither to be bought nor sold,
How wisdom, than the finest gold
   Is more to be desired.
But never mortal man has shown
   Such wisdom as the Eastern King,
For day by day, before his throne
   Their several suits the people bring,

And while each doubtful case is tried,
    Nor pauses he, nor wavers long ;
But sifts the truth on either side,
    Dividing right from wrong.
Thus did it chance, these ears of mine
    The immortal sentence heard,
Whereof the spirit seemed divine
    That prompted every word.
For surely in a plea so fine,
Conflicting statements to combine,
And equal justice to assign,
    Mere human wit had erred.
In truth such tangled question to decide,
At man's tribunal never yet was tried ;
Nor scroll of man's tribunal can record
The doubt unravelled by such fair award.
    Behold! when to his judgment-seat
        The King went up at morning light,
    There came two harlots to his feet,
        Beseeching him to do them right

One tore her hair, and rent her veil,
    And called on heaven and earth to hear;
And one stood silent, sad and pale,
    And shook in sorrow more than fear.
'Justice! great King!' the first exclaimed,
'For thou and all thy race are shamed
    If justice be not done!
Thy servant and that woman there
Dwell in one house, one chamber share,
And each fulfilled her time, and bare
    A little living son;
But lately, turning in her rest,
Her new-born child to death she pressed,
So took the babe from off my breast
    And laid it to her own.
But when at dawn I rose to chide:
" Nay, thine the infant was that died,
And mine the living child!" she cried;
Now, therefore, let my lord decide
    Between us from the throne!'

The other raised her drooping head,
And never word but these she said:
'Nay, mine the living, thine the dead;'
    Then seemed her speech to fail.
But still the first, with urgent cry,
Made loud appeal to earth and sky,
To man below and God on high,
    That justice might prevail.
And swore by all she most revered,
The holy Temple, yonder reared,
The High Priest's vesture and his beard,
The hope she held, the doom she feared,
    Hers was the truthful tale.
Pondered the King but little space,
Then bade the nearest warrior place
    The child before him there.
'Divide me now the babe,' he said,
'In equal parts from heel to head;
Each claims the living—of the dead
    Let each be given her share!'

'The King is just as God above!'
   She vowed, who first had made her plea
The other, stirred with mother's love,
   Could only sob, 'Nay, let it be!
The suit is hers. No more I strive,
But save my little child alive!'
Then rose the King, and every word
Of his decree, on us who heard,
   Came like a voice divine.
Said he to her who spoke the last,
'Take thou the babe, and keep it fast;
   Surely the babe is thine!'
And through the place, within, without,
From all the crowd went up a shout
   That seemed to swell and ring.
In lordly streets, and lowly ways,
A note of jubilee and praise,
The note a joyful nation raise
   In honour of their King.
For with the sentence thus made known,

His people, gathering round the throne,
The royal award were fain to own,
By wisdom prompted that alone
　The grace of God could bring!"

As though his listener's very soul was stirred,
She seemed to hang entranced on every word,
With parted lips, and dewy, dreamy eyes,
That veiled a deeper feeling than surprise.
A sense of woman's thraldom drawing near,
A thrill too keen for joy, too sweet for fear,
Dashed by a maiden shame unknown till now,
That sent the life-blood up from heart to brow,
That softened all the outline of her face,
And crowned her beauty with its richest
　grace;
Till day by day that beauty lost its glow,
The light, free step, unequal fell, and slow,
The dusky cheek grew wan, and almost pale,
The weary, wistful glances told their tale,

And every change that marked her altered mien
Betrayed a wound, unstanched, because unseen.
Wild were her dreams, and in her troubled rest
So heaved, so panted her unquiet breast,
The busy palace-maidens, prone to pry,
Declared each breath she drew a love-sick sigh,
And vowed that as the fever-fit increased,
Their longing Queen looked always to the East.

But now, from lip to lip the rumour flew
That tales conceived in jest were coming true;
And neighbour meeting neighbour in the gate,
Asked why the Queen thus journeyed forth in state?
Why steeds and camels in a long array
Were filing from the walls throughout the day?
Why every steed was trapped with gold, and more,
Why bags of treasure every camel bore?
And whispered, as he drew his friend aside,
That all this pomp and splendour must betide

The Queen's departure for the East—the while
Gleamed in his lean, dark face a cunning smile
While yet the talk was rife in every mouth,
Left her domains that mistress of the South;
And through the trackless desert, day by day,
Now hopeful, now depressed, she made her way,
Bound for the Holy City, there to fling
Herself, her troubles, all she had to bring,
Before the footstool of its famous King.
Judge for herself the glory and the state
Of him whom wondering travellers called the
    Great,
In rapture marking, rather than surprise,
How fair his person, and his words how wise;
And so, enchained by sense of ear and eye,
Sink to a vassal, from a royal ally,
Desirous only at his feet to fall,
And offer camels, maidens, crown, and all.
Thus did she pass where gathered nations trod
The threshold of that Temple reared to God;

And standing thus beneath the ancient beam,
To learn its history, scared as in a dream,
So strange the tales she heard, the sights she saw,
Fainted her longing soul with very awe;
And to the kingly presence drawing near,
Failed all her woman's heart in reverend love and fear.

THE BEAM.

PART III.

THE RAGE OF THE HEATHEN.

STILL, year by year, and day by day,
    While men and nations passed away,
        The holy Temple stood,
And still, to fence its inner shrine,
Fulfilling thus the task divine,
Across its porch, in level line,
        Was laid the sacred wood.
But, day by day, and year by year,
Untouched by love, untaught by fear,
The people seemed to persevere

In deeds of wrath and wrong.
God's justice seemed to incite and dare,
As striving hourly to outwear
His mercy, willing to forbear,
    His patience suffering long.
For, race by race, transgressing kings
Went lusting after evil things,
Athirst for those forbidden springs
    Idolatry that poured.
The guilt of each succeeding reign,
Nor priest, nor elder, could restrain,
And prophets thundered, all in vain,
    Threats, flouted or ignored.
While round the calf of molten gold,
An idol shameful to behold,
With rites too hideous to be told,
Men danced and worshipped as of old,
    And all forgot the Lord.
Thus Egypt, and his countless race,
Came up to spoil the holy place,

And with accursed hand
Made havoc in the sacred store,
The gold from scroll and tablet tore,
And took the golden shields, and bore
    The plunder to his land.
Nor shamed it Judah's craven king,
The dues he owed his God to bring,
When to the dark Assyrian wing
    He crept in abject fear.
Vain was the sacrilege, and vain
The impious bribe such help to gain!
The dark Assyrian in disdain
Took all, but bade his host refrain
    From aid with bow and spear.
And thus of gem and golden gleam,
Bare as the rock that stems a stream,
In rugged strength, that ancient beam
    Remained for many a year.
Till came the Heathen in his might
Of countless columns, day and night,

And pushed his spears from height to height.
And wheeled his horsemen left and right,
    In thousands from the rear.
Sore on the vexed and weary land
He laid his heavy mastering hand;
So close he knit the iron band,
None could escape it nor withstand;
    And thus the end drew near.

For now, with guilty daring, high and low
Filled for themselves the cup of wrath and woe,
Forgot their parted brethren, and ignored
Their rival's judgment, chastened of the Lord—
Samaria, but a little bolder grown
In sins but little grosser than their own,
That like a harlot had defiled her name,
Abjured her faith, and crowned herself with shame;
To hanker after gods of stone and wood,
And worship each by each in varying mood.
To raise in many a grove and open space
The standard and the symbol of disgrace;

On many an altar plighting thus her troth
To Nebo, Moloch, Baal, and Ashtaroth;
Bowed impious knees before the planets seven,
Kissed impious hands to adore the queen of Heaven,
And passed her little children through the flame,
In impious praise of Moloch's hateful name.
But who, of all she worshipped, foul or fair,
Princes, and powers of darkness and the air,
Came down to offer succour in her strait
When thundered the Assyrian at the gate?
Prone at her feet fell Dagon on his face,
Unmoved the lordly Baal kept his place,
Sweet Ashtaroth with bright and cruel smile
Looked coldly, calmly, out of Heaven the while,
And hideous Moloch, of the stony heart,
In rigid laughter carven, grinned apart.
Fain to her early faith had she returned,
Her very soul, in stress of anguish, burned;
Fain had she bared once more the conquering sword,
To battle-cry of Gideon and the Lord!

Too late! The day of grace was past and dead,
Her priests were scattered and her people fled,
Her mighty ones were fallen, her warriors slain,
Her altars soiled and trampled, while in vain
She clanked in sullen fear a captive's chain.
No hope from Heaven above nor earth below—
Woe to Samaria! and to Israel woe!

False gods! 'Tis ever thus when man abjures
The angel's guidance, for the demon's lures;
When from the straight and narrow path he strays,
To hunt a pleasant sin through pleasant ways.
Scarce can he grasp the phantom ere 'tis gone!
To take another shape, and tempt him on.
Like Moloch cruel, and like Ashtaroth fair,
Melts in its turn that other shape to air.
In vain he halts, his footsteps to retrace,
Behold! around him looms a desert place,
Seamed with a thousand paths, that in his haste
Serve but to plunge him deeper in the waste;

While all those forms that showed by day so bright,
Grown dark and hideous in the shade of night,
Around him shriek and soar, in mocking rings,
Flout with their tongues, and buffet with their wings;
'Till blinded, baffled, weary, spent, and sore,
He lies as lies the weed upon the shore,
That waves have mangled, that the storm hath tossed—
And thus a life is gone—a soul is lost!

  Warned by Samaria's downfall to refrain
From Israel's guilt—but warned, alas! in vain—
Her sister Judah followed none the less
The example of rebellion and excess;
Chose with the Heathen her unhallowed lot,
Her faith dishonoured, and her God forgot,
From no enormity of sin forbore,
A harlot, like her sister, at the core;
Yet, than her sister less depraved and vile,
That, though she cherished she deplored her guile.
And when through echoing streets her prophets went,
With dust-besprinkled brows and garments rent,

To raise the burden of their threatening cry,
In jealous wrath for Him they served on high,
Deep in her heart with each familiar word
Some gentler, purer, holier memory stirred;
For still the vain false heart that memory kept,
And though she scoffed, she sighed, and while she sinned,
  she wept!
 In vain, transgressing all alike—
  Prince, peasant, prophet, priest—
 The avenger's arm was raised to strike
  The greatest as the least—
Was none could keep his impious hand
  From off the accursed thing.
And thus the Curse was on the land,
  The people and the king—
The curse, that many a deed had earned
  Of darkness and disgrace;
The curse, repentance might have turned
  From such repentant race—
For humbled hearts, and garments rent,

And faces sad and pale,
And strength in prayer and fasting spent,
   With mercy shall prevail.
Since He who made, is loth to kill,
And loves his rebel children still,
   And listens for their cry.
Will they but pause one moment's space,
Turn but one look to meet his face,
Plead but a single word for grace,
   Be sure they shall not die!
For this, glad tidings have been sent,
That man need only to repent,
And God in mercy will relent,
   Nor count the cancelled sin.
For this, do pitying angels wait
Expectant at the Golden Gate,
Let him but knock, however late,
   To lead the suppliant in.
Alas! that still perverse in mind
To evil courses still inclined,
His ears are deaf, his eyes are blind.

Again, and yet again,
The angel whisper falls unheard,
Unmarked the angel wings are stirred,
And pleading glance and warning word
　　Are sent from heaven in vain.
Till rises the avenging day,
The sword is bared to smite and slay;
Fain would he seek the homeward way,
　　But lo! a lion there.
Like one entangled in a net,
By helpless doubt and vain regret,
And foes and fears, he stands beset,
　　To perish in despair.
Such was the fate of Judah, such the fate
Of men and nations who repent too late.
Yet not unwarned do men and nations fall.
Rang in the people's ears a prophet's call;
A prophet sent by Mercy from on high,
Charged but to ask in vain, "Why *will* **ye**
　　die?"

Scorned, disbelieved by rulers clothed in sin,
Though now the dark Assyrian hemmed them in,
Though, roaming aimless on uncertain feet,
Pale Famine gasped and glared in every street;
Though bank on bank against the city cast
Foretold the assault that must prevail at last;
Though broken as a reed, on which depends
The weak and trusting hand it only rends,
False Egypt marching, succour to bestow,
Fled like the wind before her ancient foe,
Nor halted till she reached her watery plain,
Nor sent a single horseman forth again;
Though treachery lurked within, and fear and doubt,
While drew the siege its iron girth without;
Though hideous tales, at every corner told,
Of lust and rapine made the blood run cold;
Though women, all unsexed, with bosoms bare,
And hollow wolfish eyes and matted hair,
Raved through the barren market, calling down
God's vengeance on their own beleaguered town,

And plucked their infants from the breast, and swore
There, in his face, to slay the babes they bore,
While hurling curses on the monarch's head,
Who heard his people cry in vain for bread:—
Yet none believed but Peace would be restored,
Nor deemed their prophet prompted by the Lord,
Nor stirred a hand to save him from his fate,
When angry elders hauled him to the gate,
And bade their cowering King confirm the doom
That plunged him guiltless in a living tomb.
By all but God forgotten, many a day
In mire and filth and darkness there he lay;
While, fainter grown at every trumpet call,
Weak hearts were mustering on a crumbling wall;
While War, with brawny arm, and lusty shout,
Unfurled his blood-red banner from without;
Though failing voices told, amidst the din,
How the pale flag of Sickness hung within,
And gaunt-eyed Hunger warned his brother Fear,
In ghostly whispers, how the end was near!

Then came a tawny eunuch to the King,
And pleaded hard for leave that he might bring
The prophet out, and spoke his master fair,
And urged him, lest the man should perish there;
For all the town was pinched for want, he said,
And who would think to give a captive bread?
Yielded his lord, and to the prisoner's den
He bade him lead a guard of thirty men:
And "Take me out this prophet!" was his cry,
" Go, take me out the prophet, ere he die!"

The Ethiop heard—to hear was to obey—
And gladly to the dungeon made his way,
And bade its fainting inmate nothing fear,
Confiding in his friendly succour near;
And looped beneath his arms a padded cord
To draw him forth, who trusted in the Lord!
And thus restored him from the loathsome place
To stand before the monarch, face to face.

Inflamed with zeal, with holy ardour fired,
The prophet raised his voice as one inspired,

Nor deigned, at such a time, to speak a lie,
Nor quenched, in such a plight, his warning cry.
" Thus hath the God of hosts," he said, " revealed:
If to the dark Assyrian thou shalt yield,
And go before him, shorn of all thy state,
To lead him in a conqueror through the gate—
Because my word thou seekest to obey,
Thy life will I restore thee for a prey,
And spare thine house, and all that with thee take
The captive's bitter portion, for thy sake,
Nor to avenging flames thy city give;
Thus art thou safe, and thus thy soul shall live.
But if thou wilt not leave thy fenced town,
Nor bow to Babylonian princes down,
Thyself, thine house, thy people and thy land,
Will I deliver in the Assyrian's hand,
To grind beneath his heel, to burn and slay,
And into hopeless bondage lead away."
Loth was the trembling monarch to refuse,
But said—" Alas! I fear the captive Jews,

Whom in his camp the Assyrian holds in thrall,
Lest these deceive and mock me in my fall!"
Answered the prophet—" Fear them not!" he said,
" They shall not harm one hair upon thy head;
But thou, the Lord's commandment to obey,
Do as His servant bids thee—go thy way;
Or else,—behold! He shows me His design—
Thus shall he deal in wrath with thee and thine!
The women of thine house shall eunuchs bring
To stand unveiled before the Assyrian king;
These shall not fail to mock thy fate and say,
Behold! thy faithless friends have fled away,
And those who thus beguiled thee to conspire,
Have turned their backs and left thee in the mire!
Then shalt thou see thy wives and children stand
The captives of the strong Chaldæan's hand,
Led forth to heathen exile, iron-bound,
While heathens burn thy city to the ground.
And thou the cause! Behold the sentence read!
The burden now must rest upon thy head."

Trembled the king, and bade the seer disclose
These words of doom to neither friends nor foes;
And if the Princes questioned, to declare
He had but left the prison with a prayer
That he might not return to perish there:
And thus he held his peace, and went his way,
And thus drew near the great avenging day.

  Watchman, what of the night?
    The night is dark, the stars are dim,
    The early moon, her crescent rim
      A crescent pale and bright,
    Is resting on the foeman's mound
    That girdles all the city round,
    While trumpets, answering sound for sound,
    Are pealing o'er the foeman's ground,
      Where camps the foeman's might.
  Watchman, keep watch and ward
    With eager eye and listening ear!—
    The heathens gather far and near,
    And put their trust in bow and spear,

Habergeon, shield, and sword.
But, while they muster fierce and strong,
To vex her with a grievous wrong,
Let Judah raise her battle-song,
Assured the issue shall belong,
 In battle, to the Lord!
Again! What of the night?
A muffled stir the watchman hears,
And, where the moon-beams strike, appears
A dancing gleam of distant spears,
 That moves from height to height.
The signal flash of coming harm,
Sound, watchman, sound the shrill alarm!
Rise! men of Judah! rise and arm!
 Make ready for the fight!
Be strong! be brave! your missiles bring,—
The burning brand to smear and fling,—
The rock to heave—the stone to sling—
Stand fast—for country, home, and King!
 God shall defend the right!

But how may those who took no heed
Of God in thought, and word, and deed,
Deserve his succour at their need,
   Whom, prosperous, they ignored?
Though Judah's banner flaunts on high,
Though rises Judah's battle-cry,
While to the wall her warriors fly,
The flag shall fall, the men shall die,
   Forsaken of the Lord!
Lo! girded in unseemly haste,
With garments rent and brow defaced,
A prophet, naked to the waist,
   Is striding up and down,
To raise the sad foreboding wail
That warns the mightiest men in mail,
How bow and spear shall not avail,
How hearts shall sink and courage fail,
When curses fall from heaven like hail
   On this devoted town!
Then flits a voice from ear to ear

That whispers of destruction near,
And mastery of a nameless fear
   Unnerves the strong man's hand;
While shrieks of women fill the air,
Some beat their breasts and pluck their hair,
And some, in frenzy of despair,
Can only gasp a frantic prayer
   To perish where they stand,
And still the crescent moon on high
Moves through a calm untroubled sky!

   And still on earth below,
Like waves that with a sullen roar
Break ceaseless on a troubled shore,
Higher and higher, more and more,
Swells the advancing tide of war,
   The onset of the foe.
For, one by one, to storm and hold
   The outworks, till it gained them all,
The assailing force had onward rolled
   Its columns to the city wall.

Like locusts on a field of green,
    Like spread of a devouring flame,
Without a pause or space between,
    Those swarms of heathen horsemen came;
And comrade with his comrade vied,
For each was fain the assault to guide,
    To rive and rend and slay;
And all were thirsting spoil to win,
And all were panting to begin—
Like forest wolves that gather in
    To tear a forest prey.
But now there rose a warning cry
From post to post, that rang on high,
    And seemed to mount and swell,
Till, reaching up to heaven, it made
Its wild appeal for heavenly aid,—
    Though answered by a yell
That mocked the anguish of its prayer,
That mocked the voice of its despair,—
For shapes in armour flashing, where

The fire-brand reddened all the air,
Came leaping in athwart the glare
   Like very fiends from hell!
As sweeps a torrent o'er its fall,
They swept across the battered wall,
   And through the breaches poured
In countless thousands, band by band,
The warriors of a warlike land,
And all who fell into their hand
   They put them to the sword.
Behold, throughout that blood-stained night
Of slaughter rather than of fight,
The heathen revelled in his might,
While turned and broke in shameful
   flight
   The people of the Lord.
Laughed grim Sharezer in his beard;
And Nergal smiled, and Nebo jeered;
While pointed Rabsaris, where appeared
   To flush the morning sky

A dawn of paler, weaker red,
Than those dark streams his horsemen
    shed,
Whose rage the Assyrian urged and led,
That Judah where she fell and bled,
  Beneath his heel might lie.
And fiercer than the Eastern flame
That scorched the deserts whence he came,
To wage and win his hideous game,
  The blaze he kindled here.
Already was the town aglow,
The fires were raging high and low,
While ravaged that remorseless foe
With levelled shaft and bended bow,—
  With faggot, sword, and spear.
The mother shrieked, with bosom gashed,
The babe against the stones was dashed,
With brains and blood bestrewn and splashed,
And Force was into Fury lashed
  By helplessness of Fear.

Alas! ere noon in heaven was high,
  Seemed little left to burn or slay;
Thick rolled the smoke towards the sky,
  Thick on the earth the corpses lay;
While, headlong through the farthest gate,
  Scared by the foeman's tramp and shout,
Stripped of a monarch's arms and state,
  The King of Judah galloped out.
In vain! those horses of the East,
  Not Egypt's famous race surpassed,
And soon, as the pursuit increased,
  They took the king, and bound him fast.
Before the Lord of all the Earth
  He stood in fetters, face to face
To plead the right of princely birth,
  Yet failed to win a prince's grace.
The Lord of all the Earth looked down
  In scorn and anger on his prize;
With fierce reproach and ruthless frown,
  He bade pluck out the captive's eyes.

Thus did those prophecies agree,
  That each a different tale foretold,
How Babylon he should never see,
  Yet surely should its king behold.
And thus the righteous judgment came
  On him who feared to draw the sword,
To call on the Almighty name,
  And trust in battle to the Lord.
Thus lost he, blinded and forlorn,
  His sight, his kingdom at a blow;
Thus from his side his wives were torn,
  Unveiled before a foreign foe;
And thus to heathen hands a prey,
  By heathen feet defiled and trod,
His fair and holy city lay
A smouldering heap of ashes grey,
While on that great avenging day,
In robes of flame had passed away
  The Temple of his God!
But, ere the fire had done its worst,

Those very heathen hands accursed
　　Had spoiled the sacred shrine:
The holy veil they plucked and tore,
The holy vessels outward bore,
And trampled all the holy floor
To smite the holy servants sore,
　　And spill their blood like wine.
It seemed that for a house of prayer
They entertained nor fear nor care,
Rejoicing every crime to dare,
From no pollution to forbear,
Nor aught to reverence, aught to spare,
　　Of human or divine.
Thus, leaping to the Temple's height,
The flames in their resistless might,
　　Engulphed it at a bound;
When, blazing like a kindled torch,
The goodly beam that spanned the porch,
　　Came crashing to the ground;
Till, downward by the assailants rolled,

Who laughed, yet cursed it to behold
The showers it shed of molten gold,
   A resting-place it found
Low in the pool, where day by day
Men washed the sheep they brought to slay,
Imbedded in the yielding clay,
Like some exhausted thing that lay
   Part stranded, partly drowned.

Abandoned now by friends and foes,
The conquerors these, the captives those,
While morning after morning rose,
About the city seemed to close,
   Unbroken by a sound,
Such horror as our fancies spread
About the stillness of the Dead,
The horror of a nameless dread,
   Where Silence reigns around!

BOOK V.

THE POOL.

BOOK V.

THE POOL.

YEAR after year, as day succeeded day,
  Age after age, as year succeeded year,
  Still in this turbid pool neglected lay
The beam by heathen malice grounded here.
Another race from bondage had returned;
  A warlike king sat firm upon the throne;
Smiled from the ashes of a city burned
  A fairer pile of marble and of stone.
A second Temple on the holy site
  Reared to the Syrian skies its roof of gold;
Bright shone the gilded capitals, and bright
  Flashed the tall gilded columns as of old.

Through many a year did Judah gnaw the chain
   Of bitter thraldom in a foreign land,
And looked for a deliverer in vain,
   To break the mastery of her tyrant's hand:
A coming king of more than mortal birth,
   Invested with the sceptre and the sword,
A ruler over all the bounds of earth,
   A conquering captain, an imperious lord:
Small heed she took of His celestial sway,
   From heaven who bids the dews of Mercy fall,
Whom angels in their holy home obey,
   Whose reign is Peace, goodwill, and hope for all.
Surely for this, from day-break till its close,
   True to their Master, jealous for his name,
Through every street the prophet's warning rose,
   Through every street its burden was the same:
" Repent, my people, ere the time be past!
   Repent, and turn ye from the evil thing!
The Lord of Hosts, He shall prevail at last!
   The God of Jacob, He shall be your king!

Will ye not know Him when He cometh down?
   Will ye deny the Man of Sorrows here?
Plait for his gracious brows the martyr's crown,
   Scoff at his cruel pangs with mock and jeer?
Ye fools, and blind! Come back unto the Lord,
   And turn ye to the light, while yet 'tis day!
Nor spurn the Prince by Heaven and Earth adored,
   Nor scorn the power that Heaven and Earth obey!
Such was the voice inspired, and such the cry
   That fell unmarked on Judah's graceless ear;
Such was the pledge of Him who cannot lie,
   Redeemed through many a long forbearing year
Of sins repeated, and of grace renewed,
   Of merciful reprieve from time to time,
That cleansed the guilty hands with blood imbrued
   That salved in guilty hearts the wounds of crime.
And he whom King of kings the nations called,
   Was led to favour thus the captive race;
Freed from the bonds in which they lay enthralled,
   Once more to flourish in their ancient place;

Once more to build a house unto the Lord,
   The rites their early faith required to hold,
Once more the Daily Sacrifice restored
   In homage to Jehovah, as of old:
The creatures, lent for use of man to slay,
   Prefiguring thus by man to slaughter led
The Lamb of God, who in a coming day
   Should bear a world's transgressions on his head.
But ere these victims to the steel were brought,
   As ordered by the priest's appointed rule,
The priestly servants in their course were taught
   To drive them forth and wash them in a pool,—
Hereafter, for the virtues it revealed,
   "Bethesda" or "the House of Mercy" named
The halt, the sick, the maimed, its waters healed;
   Halt, sick, and maimed its kindly powers proclaim,
Lo! here forgotten and imbedded lay
   The beam that once sustained so rich a freight,
And bore a silent witness, day by day,
   To all the changing turns of Judah's fate.

For Judah, like a fair and regal dame,
  Drew many a dread admirer to her court;
And some with smile and flattering whisper came,
  And some declared their suit with threatening port:
From him, insatiate, with ambition fired,
  The Macedonian, of prophetic birth,
Who, other worlds to subjugate desired,
  And chafed, restricted by the bounds of earth,
Down to the haughty Roman, who appeared
  Girt with a host that conquered where they trod,
The offerings of her worship, who revered,
  Nor dared to spoil the Temple of her God.
Thus did she stand again in rich array,
  A queen, enthroned by force of shield and sword
Beneath that crafty ruler's iron sway,
  Who served the Cæsar while he praised the Lord!
Who fenced her in with many a warlike line,
  And crowned her walls with many a stately tower,
And held his peace, and nursed his own design,
  Nor grudged the tribute that confirmed his power.

A man by nature moulded to command,
  In dark intrigue to bear the darker part,
A man of reckless will, and ruthless hand,
  Resistless courage and remorseless heart.
For this, ere yet his aims he had attained,
  Submission to imperial Rome he made;
Thus from imperial Rome dominion gained,
  And kept the throne she gave him, with the blade.
For this, he spared not servant, son, nor friend
  Who crossed his purpose, or his secrets knew;
But, (used alone for furtherance of his end,)
  The man whom most he trusted, him he slew,
And doomed the wife,—who lay upon his breast,
  The wife he loved,—with fierce and cruel pain,
To death, unpardoned, even as the rest,
  Nor felt one moment's ease of mind again!
How oft the glorious beauty he recalled,
  The loving, lustrous glance, the queenly brow,
The woman's smile, that all the man enthralled.
  The woman's tender graces, perished now

For bleeding Love avenged its injured right,
    And phantoms passed before his sleepless eye,
While, in the silent watches of the night,
    Rose to the echoing roof a raging cry,—
The echoing roof gave back that fatal word,
    And "Mariamne!" rang through all the air,
Till those who woke, to tremble as they heard,
    Believed a soul from hell was shrieking there.
Woe to the heart that mercy never knew!
    That beat for lust of power and pride alone,
With each succeeding crime that fiercer grew,
    And hardened in impunity to stone.
Woe to the hand, those infants' blood that shed!
    The guiltless blood, that ere the babes were cold
Cried out to heaven for vengeance on his head
    Who feared the new-born King his seers foretold.
But Woe and Vengeance seemed to tarry long,
    As careless of a people's fear and hate;
And still the monarch prospered and was strong,
    And Judah's Herod still was called the Great!

For laws of God and man while he defied,
    Hers was his highest thought, his deepest scheme,
He decked her as a tyrant decks his bride.
    And Judah's Glory still was Herod's dream.
Thus for his own and for his country's good
    The splendid monarch robed her fair and fine,
Re-built the ancient Temple where it stood,
    And hung with offerings all its holy shrine.
For this it may be Heaven looked down to spare,
    And granted leisure to repent in time,
Lest haply force of fasting and of prayer
    Might win a pardon for that life of crime.
Yet paused he not upon the downward way,
    To work of lust and murder seasoned now;
His blood ran fiercer as his locks turned grey,
    And years engraved their sins upon his brow;
Till, at the last, in anguish racked and torn,
    A living, loathsome mass, with death to cope,
He laid him down, and gnashed his teeth in scorn,
    And died, as dies a dog—without a hope.

Not his the trust that stifles earthly fear,
   Not his the faith that in affliction's hour
Beholds the Good Physician drawing near,
   And leaves its wounds to Mercy's healing power:
Like theirs, the sick and maimed, with scars and sores,
   With festering limbs corrupt, and bones laid bare,
Who thronged about Bethesda's pool by scores
   To wait the troubling of the waters there,—
Some in the porches calmly lay at rest,
   The porches five, about the place that stood,—
And some with weak, impatient gestures, pressed
   And pushed their like aside in fretful mood.
For ever and anon, they passed the word
   From lip to lip throughout the ghastly band,
That now to healing power the pool was stirred
   By virtue of the expected angel's hand;
And those who hastened down to bathe them first,
   For every ill that vexed them, solace found,
And, cured of all the woes disease had nursed,
   Stepped from the troubled surface whole and sound

With life and strength renewed, to go their way.
   Pain, sorrow, sickness vanished like a dream,
Nor guessed the secret of their welfare lay
   Wrapped in the worth of that half-sunken beam
Which peered above the lapping, shallow wave,
   To yield its balm for every human ill—
Type of the godlike power that came to save,
   The godlike mercy, unexhausted still.
Warped were the wasted forms that gathered here
   With shaking limbs and faces drawn and wan,
And dry, white lips agape, but not with fear,—
   For fear finds little room when hope is gone,—
Pointed with palsied arm the uncertain hand,
   Wagged with a palsied roll the shaking head,
The palsied feet could scarce make shift to stand,
   Through palsied veins the blood ran numbed and
      dead.
Each form of suffering helplessness could wear
   Expressed itself in wail and gasp and moan,
Yet grudged for others' pangs one sigh to spare,
   Nor seemed to credit aught except its own!

But those about the pond who thronged and pressed,
    Their helpless brethren trampled where they lay.
Soon as the water heaved its troubled breast
    The stronger pushed the weaker wretch away:
Was none would move a finger for the aid
    Of crippled fellow-sufferer far or near,
And care of self at every turn betrayed
    That self, however loathsome, still was dear!
While peevish spite seemed powerless to refrain
    From angry curse and cuff when jibed or crossed.
Thus was the task affliction set, in vain,
    And thus the teaching of their trials lost.
Yet still like precious dews from heaven that fall
    On good and bad, impartial, soft and mild,
Those gracious waters healed the plagues of all,
    And cleansed the leper, even as the child;
For Mercy takes no thought of rank or state,
    The poorest and the weakest, and the worst
Of weary souls are welcome at her gate;
    And those who stoop the lowliest, enter first.

Surely it seems not much that she requires—
   A homeless hopeless heart, a humble cry,
A spirit mourning for its dead desires,
   Yet in its desolation, loth to die.
Not much of frail mortality to ask,
   A few weak steps along the path of right;
Nor seems the Lord severe, nor hard the task,
   His yoke is easy, and his burden light.
Yet man will choose the yoke that galls him sore,
   The burden he can find no strength to bear;
These drag him down to rise again no more,
   Though both would vanish with a single prayer.
And rather will he labour, heart and hand,
   To serve a mocking master day by day,
Who laughs to see him spinning ropes of sand,
   The devil's agent, for the devil's pay,
Than earn, in easy toil, the rich reward
   Awaiting all who will but persevere,
Who weave the strands of Faith into a cord
   That holds them fast to heaven when sinking here.

Not till each earthly hope hath passed away,
    Till things of earth are fading from our sight,
We learn that those who thus misuse the day,
    Have lost their shelter from the fall of night.
Then, daunted by the Horror drawing near,
    Its vague and boundless gloom we quail to mark,
Numbed by the palsy of a nameless fear,
    Like children waking helpless in the dark.
Yet is there help if we will only seek
    The ear that listens for our faintest cry,
The hand that loves to raise the fall'n and weak,
    The voice that bids us turn before we die,
Needs but to lie, the scorn of trampling feet,
    An outcast from the flock, forlorn, alone.
Though scarce the poor lost lamb has strength to bleat,
    The Shepherd stoops to claim it for his own,
And lifts it with a kind and gentle hand,
    And heals it with a touch from shame and sin,
And bears it homeward to the happy land,
    Where pain and sorrow shall not enter in.

Thus, when the world has crushed him to the dust,
    When all he asks is death to make an end,
Pierced by the reed whereon he leaned in trust,
    Behold the sinner's refuge and his Friend!

Now when the angel to Bethesda came
    And moved the water, round its margin drew
Their trailing limbs the impotent and lame,
    With rags and filth defiled, a hideous crew.

And in the loathsome pressure, one of these,
    Without a friendly hand his steps to stay,
By torture urged, while hindered by disease,
    Sank to the earth, exhausted where he lay—

While those who should have held a brother dear,
    Scourged by a like affliction of their own,
Turned from his sufferings with a brutal jeer,
    And mocked the very pangs themselves had known

And those whose manhood might have served his need
    A neighbour or a kinsman, had in care
Plight so forlorn, why should they help or heed?
    They knew him not—so let him perish there.

Consumed and sapped by many a year of pain,
    Thus from the pool he turned a hopeless eye,
And looked to heaven and earth for aid in vain,
    And wept, because it seemed so hard to die
A lonely sufferer, in a suffering band,
    A friendless waif, where friends were thronging round,
A helpless wretch, though help was close at hand,
    By God and man forsaken, on the ground.
But ere his reeling senses failed him quite,
    Behold! he knew a gracious Presence near:
A gracious vision passed before his sight,
    A gracious form bent down to soothe and cheer.
Thrilled to his heart the accents all divine,
    "Would'st thou not fain be healed and whole, my son?"
"Master," he said, "for trouble such as mine,
    Friend, hope or succour, surely can be none!
Lo! when the pool is stirred, and I would lave
    My tortured limbs, will no man draw me nigh?
Kind hands are stretched by scores the rest to save,
    But I am left, uncared for, here to die!"

Answered in gracious words the gracious voice,
    Words that a balm and cordial seemed to shed,
That bade his strength return, his heart rejoice:
    "Rise up, and take thy bed and walk," it said.
Then rose he, in an instant, whole and sound,
    And, lifting up the bed whereon he lay,
Regardless of the Jews who murmured round
    That thus he broke the Sabbath, went his way.
For life came glowing back while yet he heard
    The godlike tones that life and hope conveyed.
Healed by the virtue of a single word—
    "Take up thy bed and walk!"—the man obeyed.
Enough for him the glad result to feel;
    The Master's will he little cared to learn,
Nor asked why here he came on earth to heal,
    Nor sought to give him worship in return.
Though in the Temple, when he saw again
    That face divine, he could not but recall
His holy name, who eased the throb of pain,
    And bade him "Sin no more, lest worse befall!"

Who flings a starving dog one scrap of meat,
    Or binds a rag about its wounded limb,
Beholds the creature crawling to his feet
    And lifting grateful eyes alone to him.
For lower instincts loftier aims attain,
    The poorer nature yields the richer fruit,
And Reason, in her proudest mood, may gain
    A true and touching lesson from the brute.
We find no love for One who loves us best;
    We learn no trust, where most we should depend;
But lock our fealty in rebellious breast,
    And scorn to own a master in a friend.
The dog will fawn on him who helped its need,
    And lick the kindly hand that gave the bone,
Bound to its lord by one such gracious deed.
    Ingratitude belongs to man alone;—
Ingratitude! that springs a plant accursed,
    From favoured fields where showers of mercy fall,
To bear a poisoned fruit—if not the worst,
    The vilest, basest sin among them all!

Of man's transgression, first and instant cause,
    That doomed his race eternally to die
Till Justice set aside her primal laws,
    And Mercy gave redemption from on high.
Redemption, man's defiance can refuse
    In wilful folly when he turns away,
The darker paths of sin and shame to choose
    That lead him downward from the light of day,
To sink at length in everlasting deeps,
    Through everlasting regions of despair,
Where memory ceases not, nor conscience sleeps,—
    The fire unquenched, the worm undying there!
An upward path he takes no thought to find,
    The stream he scorns that runs to cleanse his guile,
And man is lost because his eyes are blind,
    And man is lost because his heart is vile.
Oh! for the loving instinct, that would seek
    Its shelter in the home that gave it birth;
Oh! for the lowly wisdom of the meek,
    Blessed by their Master as the heirs of earth.

Oh! for the faith that Master to receive,
   On Him to lay our load and cast our care;
The faith that bids us act as we believe,
   Removing mountains by the force of prayer.
Alas! that like the Jews, on outward form
   We hope to rear the stronghold of our trust,
And when the winds arise, and beats the storm,
   Behold! our fabric crumbles into dust.
Alas! that when we strive to thread again
   The sinful maze wherein we loved to stray,
A hand to guide us forth we seek in vain,
   The Saviour has " conveyed himself away."
Not even thus our hearts should wholly fail—
   None so forlorn but He will heed their prayer.
We need but plead in earnest to prevail,
   And seek the Temple—we shall find Him there.
This is the gracious promise that He gave,
   The faithful pledge of Him who cannot lie,
Whose mission here was not to slay, but save:
   " Where two or three are gathered—there am I "—

Linked in the human bond of brother's love,
    When two or three shall pray with one accord,
Borne straightway to the Mercy Seat above,
    That prayer shall find acceptance with the Lord
And angels day by day from heaven descend
    To watch the pool of succour here below.
Are none, for lack of kinsman or of friend,
    Need perish by the margin where they flow;
These ministers shall prompt the saving word,
    And where the healing waters lap and toss,
Shall bid him mark how through the surface stirred,
    Appears the sacred figure of the Cross.
Then sinking, yielding to the oppressor's might,
    Though heaven itself seem loth its aid to give,
Needs but on this to fix his failing sight,
    The man is saved—For he who looks shall live.

BOOK VI.

THE CENTURION.

BOOK VI.

THE CENTURION.

THE level rift that dawn reveals,
   Is widening, cold and clear,
    And through the sedge a whisper steals,
And in the camp a trumpet peals,
   To tell that day is near.
Though fenced be that encampment round,
With ditch and rampart, bank and mound,
The Legion, holding conquered ground,
   Has pushed an outpost here,
Where, from the West, the Danube flows,
   To find his Euxine home,

Where from the North, the tempest blows,
To bend the woods, and drive the snows,
Where swarm the fierce and rugged foes,
  Who hate the name of Rome,
For every foot has cost her dear,
  And every foot she holds in ward,
Won by the might of sword and spear,
  Kept by the right of spear and sword:
With even foot and measured pace,
  Advance her columns, sure and slow,
From clime to clime, from place to place,
  Absorbing nations as they go.
Subduing, quelling all alike,
  Of those who yield, or turn at bay:
Where once the cruel talons strike,
  Her eagles never loose their prey.
To plant her eagles far and wide,
  Expending wisdom, valour, worth,
She sees the warriors die, with pride,
  Who make her mistress of the earth.

THE CENTURION.

For this, the Roman trumpets sound,
    Wherever living thing draws breath.
For this, the Legion takes its ground,
    For this, defends it to the death,
For this, a forward outpost placed,
    The Legion's movements checks and guides,
Where through the broad and stagnant waste
    The broad and sluggish river glides.
And here, in garments soiled and torn,
And arms that many a dint have borne,
    Roused from his lair of slush and mire,
A soldier, scarred and battle-worn,
Is musing in the chilly morn
    Before a dying fire.

His watch is over; ear and eye
    May rest them for a space,
And sadly from the brightening sky
    He turns a darkened face;

And stretches numbed and stiffened hands
    Such failing warmth to meet
As lingers in the smouldering brands
    That whiten at his feet.
Of moaning wind, and bending reed,
    And cheerless gleam of early day,
His senses take but little heed,
    And all his thoughts are far away.
For where the flame has sunken low,
    Ere yet his limbs are scarcely warmed,
The embers, in their parting glow,
    The figure of a Cross have formed.
And, like a vision of the night,
    That holds the haunted sleeper fast,
Arise to scare his troubled sight,
    The phantoms of an awful Past.
Again, with shield and spear, he stands,
    A rock amidst a raging sea
Of scowling brows and tossing hands,
    That point the way to Calvary.

Again he hears the tempest swell,
    Of hungry hate, in howl and groan,
The savage laugh, the hideous yell
    Of murder, slaked by blood alone.
And if the tumult waxes high,
    Disdains to notice, calm and proud,
But with a soldier's scornful eye
    Reviews the loose disordered crowd,
And thinks how masterly and well
    With spears and bow-men twenty score
The rising he could crush and quell,
    Nor ask a single helmet more!
Yet wonders in his heart, that he
    Who governs in the conquered town
Endures this brawling rout to see,
    Nor stirs to put the riot down;
Although, but now, at break of day,
    His judgment when the accusers sought,
Himself had heard that Ruler say,
    No fault he found in Him they brought,

But held Him innocent and just,
    A blameless man, devoid of guile,
Yet pandered to a people's lust
    By sending Him to death, the while.
Though chief of but a hundred men,
    A mere Centurion, then as now,
The flush of anger, now as then,
    Is rising in his swarthy brow,
For hate of that presumptuous race
    Who dared assume judicial power.
Soon had they fled before the face
So pure and princely in its grace,
Could *he* have filled the Prætor's place,
    If only for an hour!
Of Rabbi, Scribe, and written law,
    But little did he know or care,
Believed alone in things he saw,
    And trusted harness more than prayer;
Had lively faith in proven steel,
    When wielded by a practised hand,

But moral force could scarcely feel,
   Nor moral doubts could understand,
Nor patience found for those, nor ruth,
   Who loved on dogmas to refine,
And to the question,—" What is truth ? "—
Had learned to answer from his youth,
   " A thousand men in line ! "
But now, while that tumultuous press
   Was surging round a single form,
In candour could not but confess
   That He, who faced so wild a storm
With gracious and forgiving mien,
   That rather seemed to grieve than fear,
Displayed a courage too serene
   And god-like, to be earth-born here.
And when they sought Bethesda's pool,
   And drew the beam from out its wave,
To shape it by the ghastly rule
   That forms a gibbet for a slave,
And bade the scared Cyrenian bear

His hideous burden in the van,
　To guide the grim procession there
　　That led to death the Son of Man—
Lo! while the slave, his shoulders brown,
　That awful emblem to up-rear,
Stripped to the waist, and girt his gown,
Dark was the stern centurion's frown,
Fain had he struck the caitiff down
　With handle of his spear!
But meekly, solemnly, and slow,
　The while He passed along,
There peered from every nook a foe,
And threatened every hand a blow,
On every side from high and low
　Poured insult, wrath, and wrong;
Derisive shouts and brutal cries,
On Him, who walked in gentle guise,
With placid brow, and patient eyes,
Where Love eternal seemed to rise,
　Through that blaspheming throng.

What could he do but turn aside,
The scorn and shame he felt to hide?
His conscience pricked, his heart rebelled,
The soldier's pride within him swelled,
And half in pity, half in ire,
He thirsted with a fierce desire
To see the Prætor lift his hand,
In sign he might advance his band,
And sweep this Jewish rabble clear
With pointed shaft, and levelled spear.
How humbly in that open space,
Then had he sought the gracious face,
And craved permission but to fall
And worship in the sight of all!
Not so—the instincts of his trade,
The very hilt that crossed his blade,
The eagle on his golden crest,
Were but as symbols to attest
That soul and body, life and limb,
Belonged to Cæsar, not to him;

And right or wrong, at best or worst
His duty was to Cæsar first.

Have we not each a Cæsar of our own,
Whose rule can brook no rival near the throne?
A despot claiming undivided sway,
Whom reason, heart, and conscience must obey;
Who draws his tribute to the utmost mite,
Nor bates a jot of his accustomed right?
Who day by day a heavier burden lays,
And plies us harder as our strength decays,
Till crushed and sore beneath the hopeless strain,
We sink without a wish to rise again?
In every shape the tyrant works his will,
In every shape he reigns, a tyrant still:
Now like a monarch, brave in royal attire,
His lust, ambition, power his sole desire;
Not for its uses valued, but its fame,
Truth, honour, justice, bartering for a name.

Now in the mask that beauty joys to wear,
Of blushing smiles bewildering, false and fair,
A wreath of roses wearing, to conceal
The torturing pressure of a band of steel,
A coiling serpent, cooing like a dove,
The wild idolatry that men call love.
Anon, with rage of hunger uncontrolled,
Insatiate, starving for the greed of gold,
Privation, pain, accepting, but to earn
Some yellow earth, by morsels, in return.
Of all that rule us, none so base and vile
As avarice—none so absolute the while.
Or sleek and torpid, on a cushioned throne
He cares to seek indulgence, ease, alone;
Each nobler feeling stifled in its birth,
By joys of sense, that chain him to the earth;
Clogged with a sloth no effort can control,
Sunk in a hopeless slumber of the soul,
Yet fain to govern, unrestrained of will,
And jealous of supreme dominion still;

Nor stern rebuke he has, nor angry frown,
But with a leaden hand, remorseless bears us down.
Imperious masters these! and yet of all
The powers of evil holding him in thrall,
Ambition, pleasure, sloth, desire of pelf,
None press so hard on man as love of self;
For though at first his higher instincts spurn
The yoke that frets and galls at every turn,
Too soon, debased in mind, in heart depraved,
His very nature so becomes enslaved,
The spirit hath not even a desire
To rise from where it wallows in the mire;
But sunk, degraded to the last degree,
Foregoes the very longing to be free!
And this is Cæsar's service! To enrol
The mortal body, and the immortal soul,
Without a hope beyond; for Cæsar's pay,
The worthless pittance doled from day to day,
The leave to do his work, his badge to wear,
His eagles in the weary march to bear,

Wade ankle-deep in blood through fields of strife,
To forfeit in his cause a soldier's life,
And offer all to an ungracious lord
Who grudges even thanks for a reward.—
Such is the fate of those who choose to bring
Their sole allegiance to an earthly king,
Who lay their lives before an earthly throne,
And put their trust in earthly power alone,
By fear or interest blinded, who obey
The hand that cannot reach beyond to-day,
And render Cæsar, at the imperial nod,
A tribute that is only due to God!

* * * * *

    Behold! 'tis done!
Quenched is the light of heaven, and veiled the sun,
    While earthward, like a pall,
A horror of great darkness seems to fall
About a dead creation, shrouding all;
    The plain is heaving, wave on wave,
    And corpses, risen from the grave,

  Are gliding to and fro.
Great God! It scares the bravest of the brave
  To see them come and go,
With white sepulchral faces, calm and clear,
  Untouched by weal or woe,
  Unmoved by hope or fear,
And deep far-seeing eyes that know
The secrets of another world, and glow
With sad and solemn lustre, never kindled here:
  For it is finished now,—
And heaven once more has triumphed over hell—
The devils quake, remembering how they fell,
And holy angels, where with God they dwell,
  In adoration bow.
Though through the realms of bliss there rings a cry
Forced from His human half that needs must die,
To trouble all the Seraphim on high,
And stamp the brand of shame and agony
  On each immortal brow.
  While ransomed man below

Scoffs at his Saviour on the Cross,
And, rescued from eternal loss,
  Denies Him yet. Although
The sternest mood of earthly pride,
Taught by the thief, who at His side
Found grace and pardon ere he died,
Might learn to love its Friend and Guide,
  Its Lord and God to know.
Thus, as a cloud before the gales
  That freshen morning skies,
As darkness, pealing off like scales
  To clear a blind man's eyes,
The stern Centurion, watching how,
  With one expiring groan,
Death on the pure and precious brow
  Is set as on a throne,
Knows that his doubts have passed away
  Before a dawn of light,
Bewildered by the dazzling day
  His soul receives her sight;

Thrills a conviction at his heart,
    Shoots through his brain a gleam,
And like a sleeper, with a start,
    Awaking from a dream,
In fear and awe he bows his head,
    As cowers a slave beneath the rod,
And cries aloud, for very dread,
In presence of the Holy dead,
    " This was the Son of God!"

*   *   *   *   *

In hoary dust the embers lie
    To smear the oozing clay,
The flame but flickers up to die,
    The vision fleets away.
Yet for an instant, charged with light,
    That streams through heart and brain,
Pervading memory, sense, and sight,
    It flashes out again,
And seems to rise, and heave, and swim,

And sink, and disappear.
For who is this? the stranger grim,
That lays his grasp on every limb,
To hold him helpless here;
With failing hand, with fading eye,
Forbid to fight, forbid to fly,
Pinned like a log on earth to lie,
Across a useless spear.
His senses droop, he pants for breath,
—Surely the end is near,
It is not sleep, it is not fear,
It must be Death!—
Lithe is the arm that draws the bow,
Where swoops the Scythian on his foe,
And ere the singing arrow's point
Has cloven through the harness joint,
With bending form and tightened rein,
The mounted archer scours the plain,
To join a wild careering host,
And tell with savage laugh and boast,

That yonder, in the sedges, where
Last night a watch-fire shed its glare,
This morning, ere the dawn was red,
He left a Roman soldier dead!

Soon of each swift and shaggy steed
These hardy warriors taxed the speed,
    To spoil that fallen prey,
Like ruffled falcons, wheeling round;
But ere a rider touched the ground
    The Roman's soul had passed away,
Uprising in desire of light,
And swifter than their arrow's flight,
Had pierced inevitable night
    To find eternal day.

Down-struck, by an extinguished fire,
His armour soiled, with blood and mire,
    His eagle-crest defiled,
Ere yet they bent to strip him bare,

While round the dead they gathered there,
    It seemed to them he smiled.
And though he lay on Scythian soil
For Scythian foes to spurn and spoil,
    And gave his life to Rome,
Yet surely One to whom he raised
The dying thought that prayed and praised,
Stooped from the Heaven on which he gazed,
    And led his spirit Home.

THE END.

THE
Select Library of Fiction.

PRICE TWO SHILLINGS EACH.
COMPRISING
THE BEST WORKS BY THE BEST AUTHORS.

⁎ *When Ordering the Numbers only need be given.*

By ANTHONY TROLLOPE.

- 85 Doctor Thorne.
- 86 Macdermots of Ballycloran.
- 88 Rachel Ray.
- 93 The Kellys and the O'Kellys.
- 95 Tales of all Countries.
- 96 Castle Richmond.
- 100 The Bertrams.
- 122 Miss Mackenzie.
- 125 Belton Estate.
- 183 Lotta Schmidt.
- 192 An Editor's Tales.
- 203 Ralph the Heir.
- 242 La Vendee.
- 244 Lady Anna.
- 320 Vicar of Bullhampton.

- 365 Sir Harry Hotspur.
- 384 Is He Popenjoy?
- 404 An Eye for an Eye.
- 408 Cousin Henry.
- 421 Dr. Wortle's School.

2s. 6d. Vols.

- 116 Orley Farm.
- 120 Can You Forgive Her?
- 186 Phineas Finn.
- 137 He Knew He was Right.
- 243 Eustace Diamonds.
- 267 Phineas Redux.
- 362 The Prime Minister.
- 417 The Duke's Children.

By CHARLES LEVER.

- 17 Jack Hinton.
- 22 Harry Lorrequer.
- 27 The O'Donoghue.
- 32 The Fortunes of Glencore.
- 35 One of Them.
- 48 Sir Jasper Carew.
- 53 A Day's Ride: A Life's Romance.
- 54 Maurice Tiernay.
- 75 Barrington.
- 89 Luttrell of Arran.
- 193 Rent in a Cloud.
- 211 Sir Brook Fosbrooke.
- 213 The Bramleighs.
- 225 Tony Butler.
- 227 That Boy of Norcott's.

- 228 Lord Kilgobbin.
- 229 Cornelius O'Dowd.
- 372 Nuts and Nutcrackers.
- 531 Tales of the Trains.
- 532 Paul Goslett's Confessions.

2s. 6d. Vols.

- 18 Charles O'Malley.
- 20 The Daltons.
- 23 Knight of Gwynne.
- 25 Dodd Family Abroad.
- 28 Tom Burke.
- 30 Davenport Dunn.
- 33 Roland Cashel.
- 42 Martins of Cro' Martin.

By HARRISON AINSWORTH.

- 335 Cardinal Pole.
- 342 Constable of the Tower.
- 368 Leaguer of Lathom.
- 369 Spanish Match.
- 370 Constable de Bourbon.

- 371 Old Court.
- 373 Myddleton Pomfret.
- 374 Hilary St. Ives.
- 419 Lord Mayor of London.
- 420 John Law.

By HENRY KINGSLEY.

- 195 Geoffry Hamlyn.
- 196 Ravenshoe.
- 197 Hillyars and Burtons.
- 198 Silcote of Silcotes.

- 199 Leighton Court.
- 200 Austin Elliot.
- 201 Reginald Hetherege.

THE SELECT LIBRARY OF FICTION.

By WHYTE MELVILLE.

387 Tilbury Nogo.
338 Uncle John.
389 The White Rose.
390 Cerise.
391 Brookes of Bridlemere.
392 "Bones and I."

393 "M. or N."
394 Contraband.
395 Market Harborough.
396 Sarchedon.
397 Satanella.
398 Katerfelto.
399 Sister Louise.

400 Rosine.
401 Roy's Wife.
402 Black, but Comely.
410 Riding Recollections.
600 Songs and Verses.
601 The True Cross.

By Mrs. OLIPHANT.

271 May.
276 For Love and Life.
277 Last of the Mortimers.
280 Squire Arden.

285 Ombra.
295 Madonna Mary.
316 Days of My Life.
317 Harry Muir.
323 Heart and Cross.

333 Magdalene Hepburn.
334 House on the Moor.
336 Lilliesleaf.
377 Lucy Crofton.

By HAWLEY SMART.

321 Broken Bonds.
324 Two Kisses.
328 False Cards.
359 Courtship.

361 Bound to Win.
354 Cecile.
367 Race for a Wife.
375 Play or Pay.

382 Sunshine and Snow.
418 Belles and Ringers.
423 Social Sinners.

By JANE AUSTEN.

163 Sense and Sensibility.
164 Emma.
165 Mansfield Park.
166 Northanger Abbey.
167 Pride and Prejudice.

By VICTOR HUGO.

425 Jean Valjean (Les Misérables).
426 Cosette and Marius (Les Misérables).
427 Fantine (Les Misérables).
428 By the King's Command.

By MAX ADELER.

429 Out of the Hurly Burly.
430 Elbow Room.

431 Random Shots.
432 An Old Fogey.

By C. C. CLARKE.

67 Charlie Thornhill.
117 Flying Scud.
128 Crumbs from a Sportsman's Table.
139 Which is the Winner?
157 Lord Falconberg's Heir.
168 Beauclercs, Father and Son.
207 Box for the Season.

By ANNIE THOMAS.

114 Theo Leigh.
234 A Passion in Tatters.
268 He Cometh Not, She Said.
274 No Alternative.
338 Blotted Out.
376 A Laggard in Love.
412 High Stakes.

By E. P. ROE.

448 Opening of a Chestnut Burr.
449 A Face Illumined.
450 Barriers Burned Away.
451 What Can She Do?
452 A Day of Fate.

453 Without a Home.
523 A Knight of the 19th Century.
524 Near to Nature's Heart.
526 From Jest to Earnest.

By MISS E. MARLITT.

235 Old Maid's Secret.
318 Gold Elsie.
433 The Second Wife.
434 The Little Moorland Princess.

By AMELIA B. EDWARDS.

272 In the Days of My Youth.
298 Miss Carew.
304 Debenham's Vow.
307 Monsieur Maurice.

THE SELECT LIBRARY OF FICTION.

By VARIOUS AUTHORS.

- 6 My Uncle the Curate. M. W. SAVAGE.
- 11 The Half-Sisters. G. JEWSBURY.
- 12 Bachelor of the Albany. SAVAGE.
- 40 Belle of the Village. JOHN MILLS.
- 41 Charles Auchester. Author of "My First Season."
- 44 Sorrows of Gentility. G. JEWSBURY.
- 46 Jacob Bendixen, the Jew. C. GOLDSCHMIDT.
- 47 Mr. and Mrs. Asheton. Author of "Woman's Devotion."
- 50 Marian Withers. G. JEWSBURY.
- 56 The Only Child. Lady SCOTT.
- 58 Master of Hounds. "SCRUTATOR."
- 59 Constance Herbert. G. JEWSBURY.
- 66 Elsie Venner. O. W. HOLMES.
- 70 Falcon Family. M. W. SAVAGE.
- 71 Reuben Medlicott. M. W. SAVAGE.
- 72 Country Gentleman. "SCRUTATOR."
- 78 Deep Waters. ANNA DRURY.
- 79 Misrepresentation. ANNA DRURY.
- 81 Queen of the Seas. Capt. ARMSTRONG.
- 82 He Would be a Gentleman. LOVER.
- 87 Lindisfarn Chase. T. A. TROLLOPE.
- 92 Irish Stories and Legends. LOVER.
- 99 Jack Brag. THEODORE HOOK.
- 101 Faces for Fortunes. A. MAYHEW.
- 102 Father Darcy. Mrs. MARSH.
- 103 Time, the Avenger. Mrs. MARSH.
- 110 Emilia Wyndham. Mrs. MARSH.
- 127 Dumbleton Common. Lady EDEN.
- 141 Lizzie Lorton. Mrs. LINTON.
- 142 The Mad Willoughbys. Ditto.
- 146 Rose Douglas. S. W. R.
- 154 Riverston. Mrs. G. M. CRAIK.
- 159 Secret Dispatch. JAMES GRANT.
- 185 The Brothers. ANNA H. DRURY.
- 204 Semi-Attached Couple. Lady EDEN.
- 205 Semi-Detached House. Lady EDEN.
- 206 Woman's Devotion. Author of "Margaret and her Bridesmaids."
- 212 Aunt Margaret. E. F. TROLLOPE.
- 214 Ladies of Bever Hollow. ANNE MANNING.
- 230 Bernard Marsh. G. P. R. JAMES.
- 231 Charley Nugent. Author of "St. Aubyns of St. Aubyn."
- 239 Hawksview. HOLME LEE.
- 240 Gilbert Messenger. HOLME LEE.
- 241 Thorney Hall. HOLME LEE.
- 245 St. Aubyns of St. Aubyn. Author of "Charley Nugent."
- 270 Hagarene. Author of "Guy Livingstone."
- 275 Colonel Dacre. Author of "Caste."
- 278 My Son's Wife. Author of "Caste."
- 281 Lost Bride. Lady CHATTERTON.
- 284 Wild Georgie. J. MIDDLEMAS.
- 286 First in the Field.
- 287 Pearl. Author of "Caste."
- 289 The White House by the Sea. M. BETHAM EDWARDS.
- 291 Entanglements. Author of "Caste."
- 293 Oaste. Author of "Pearl."
- 294 Off the Line. Lady THYNNE.
- 295 Ladies of Lovel Leigh. Author of "Queen of the County."
- 297 Queen of the County. Author of "Three Wives."
- 299 Olympus to Hades. Mrs. FORRESTER.
- 303 Book of Heroines. Author of "Ladies of Lovel Leigh."
- 305 Fair Women. Mrs. FORRESTER.
- 309 John and I. M. BETHAM EDWARDS.
- 310 Queen of Herself. ALICE KING.
- 311 Sun and Shade. Author of "Ursula's Love Story."
- 313 Wild Flower of Ravensworth. M. BETHAM EDWARDS.
- 315 Lisabee's Love Story. Ditto.
- 325 Leyton Hall. MARK LEMON.
- 326 A Charming Fellow. E. F. TROLLOPE.
- 329 Squire of Beechwood. "SCRUTATOR."
- 343 A Fatal Error. J. MASTERMAN.
- 347 Mainstone's Housekeeper. E. METEYARD.
- 349 Mount Sorrel. Mrs. MARSH.
- 354 Off the Roll. KATHERINE KING.
- 360 Condoned. ANNA C. STEELE.
- 363 Gardenhurst. ANNA C. STEELE.
- 379 All for Greed. Baroness DE BURY.
- 380 Dr. Austin's Guests. W. GILBERT.
- 381 My Heart's in the Highlands. Miss GRANT.
- 383 Broken Toys. ANNA C. STEELE.
- 386 Kelverdale. Earl DESART.
- 409 Dark and Light Stories. M. HOPE.
- 414 Pique. Author of "Agatha Beaufort."
- 415 Chips from an Old Block. Author of "Charlie Thornhill."
- 416 Blithedale Romance. HAWTHORNE.
- 422 Tragic Comedians. G. MEREDITH.
- 424 Pickwick Papers. C. DICKENS.
- 435 No Sign. Mrs. CASHEL HOEY.
- 436 Blossoming of an Aloe. Ditto.
- 437 Evelina. Miss BURNEY.
- 438 Unrequited Affection. BALZAC.
- 439 Scottish Chiefs. JANE PORTER.

4 THE SELECT LIBRARY OF FICTION.

440 Improvisatore. H. C. ANDERSEN.
441 Arthur Bonnicastle. J. G. HOLLAND.
442 Innocents Abroad. MARK TWAIN.
443 The Squanders of Castle Squander. WM. CARLETON.
445 Never Again. W. S. MAYO.
446 The Berber. W. S. MAYO.
447 The American. H. JAMES, Jun.
454 Genevieve and The Stonemason. A. LAMARTINE.
455 Debit and Credit. GUSTAV FREYTAG.
456 The Mistress of Langdale Hall. R. M. KETTLE.
457 Smugglers and Foresters. Ditto.
458 Hillsden on the Moors. Ditto.
459 Under the Grand Old Hills. Ditto.
460 Fabian's Tower. R. M. KETTLE.
461 The Wreckers. R. M. KETTLE.
462 My Home in the Shires. KETTLE.
463 The Sea and the Moor. KETTLE.
464 Tom Cringle's Log. M. SCOTT.
465 Artemus Ward, His Book; and Travels among the Mormons.
466 Artemus Ward's Letters to Punch, and Mark Twain's Practical Jokes.
467 Leah, the Jewish Maiden.
468 Margaret Catchpole. COBBOLD.
469 The Suffolk Gipsy. COBBOLD.
470 Zana, the Gipsy. Miss STEVENS.
471 The Sailor Hero. Capt. ARMSTRONG.
472 The Cruise of the "Daring." Ditto.
473 The Sunny South. Ditto.
474 Romance of the Seas. "WATERS."
476 Poe's Tales of Mystery.
477 Wild as a Hawk. KATH. MACQUOID.
478 Margaret. SYLVESTER JUDD.
479 The Gambler's Wife. Mrs. GREY.
480 Forgotten Lives. Mrs. NOTLEY.
481 The Kiddle-a-Wink. Mrs. NOTLEY.
482 Love's Bitterness. Mrs. NOTLEY.
483 In the House of a Friend. Ditto.
484 Mountain Marriage. MAYNE REID.
485 The Conspirators. A. DE VIGNY.
486 Brownrigg Papers. DOUGLAS JERROLD.
487 Marriage Bonds. C. J. HAMILTON.
488 The Flynns of Flynnville. Ditto.
489 Paid in Full. HENRY J. BYRON.
490 Royston Gower. THOMAS MILLER.
491 Briefless Barrister. JOHN MILLS.
492 Chelsea Pensioners. G. R. GLEIG.
493 Eulalie. W. STEPHENS HAYWARD.
494 The Diamond Cross. Ditto.
495 Image of his Father. Bros. MAYHEW.
496 Twelve Months of Matrimony. EMILIE CARLEN.
497 The Brilliant Marriage. EMILIE CARLEN.
498 The Sea Lions. J. F. COOPER.
499 Mark's Reef. J. F. COOPER.
500 Man of the World. S. W. FULLOM.
501 King and Countess. S. W. FULLOM.
502 A Lease for Lives. FONBLANQUE.
503 Waverley. Sir WALTER SCOTT.
504 Kenilworth. Sir WALTER SCOTT.
505 Ivanhoe. Sir WALTER SCOTT.
506 The Antiquary. Sir WALTER SCOTT.
507 Paul Clifford. LYTTON BULWER.
508 Last Days of Pompeii. BULWER.
509 Pelham. LYTTON BULWER.
510 Eugene Aram. LYTTON BULWER.
511 Midshipman Easy. MARRYAT.
512 Japhet in Search of a Father. Captain MARRYAT.
513 Jacob Faithful. Captain MARRYAT.
514 Peter Simple. Captain MARRYAT.
515 Hector O'Halloran. W. H. MAXWELL.
516 Christopher Tadpole. A. SMITH.
517 Pic-nic Papers. Edited by CHARLES DICKENS.
518 Bret Harte's Complete Tales.
519 Shiloh. Mrs. W. M. L. JAY.
520 Holden with the Cords. Mrs. JAY.
521 Nicholas Nickleby. C. DICKENS.
522 Cruise of the Midge. M. SCOTT.
525 Odd or Even? Mrs. WHITNEY.
527 The Backwoodsman. Sir C. L. WRAXALL.
528 Almost a Quixote. Miss LEVIEN.
529 Lost and Won. G. M. CRAIK.
530 Winifred's Wooing. G. M. CRAIK.
533 Counterparts. Author of "Charles Auchester."
534 My First Season. Ditto.
535 Clover Cottage. M. W. SAVAGE.
536 Bret Harte's Deadwood Mystery, and Mark Twain's Nightmare.
537 The Heathen Chinee. BRET HARTE.
538 Wan Lee, the Pagan, &c. Ditto.
539 American Drolleries. MARK TWAIN.
540 Funny Stories and Humorous Poems. MARK TWAIN and O. W. HOLMES.
541 Mark Twain's Mississippi Pilot, and Bret Harte's Two Men of Sandy Bar.

2s. 6d. Vols.

319 Forgotten by the World. KATHERINE MACQUOID.
373 The Wizard of the Mountain. WILLIAM GILBERT.

Warwick House, Dorset Buildings,
Salisbury Square, E.C.

WARD, LOCK & CO.'S
LIST OF
STANDARD REFERENCE VOLUMES,
AND
Popular Useful Books.

Of all Works of Reference published of late years, not one has gained such general approbation as BEETON'S ILLUSTRATED ENCYCLOPÆDIA. *The importance of this valuable compilation in the cause of mental culture has long been acknowledged, and of its real usefulness to the public the most gratifying proofs have been received. It is undoubtedly one of the Most Comprehensive Works in existence, and is*

THE CHEAPEST ENCYCLOPÆDIA EVER PUBLISHED.

Complete in Four Volumes, royal 8vo, half-roan, price 42*s.*; half-calf, 63*s.*

BEETON'S
ILLUSTRATED ENCYCLOPÆDIA
OF UNIVERSAL INFORMATION.
COMPRISING
GEOGRAPHY, HISTORY, BIOGRAPHY, ART, SCIENCE, AND LITERATURE,
AND CONTAINING
**4,000 Pages, 50,000 Articles, and 2,000 Engravings
and Coloured Maps.**

In BEETON'S ILLUSTRATED ENCYCLOPÆDIA will be found complete and authentic information respecting the **Physical and Political Geography, Situation, Population, Commerce and Productions,** as well as the principal **Public Buildings** of every **Country** and important or interesting **Town in the World,** and the leading **Historical Events** with which they have been connected; concise **Biographies of Eminent Persons,** from the most remote times to the present day; brief Sketches of the leading features of **Egyptian, Greek, Roman, Oriental, and Scandinavian Mythology;** a Complete Summary of the **Moral, Mathematical, Physical and Natural Sciences;** a plain description of the **Arts;** and an interesting Synopsis of **Literary Knowledge.** The Pronunciation and Etymology of every leading term introduced throughout the Encyclopædia are also given.

"WE KNOW OF NO BOOK which in such small compass gives SO MUCH INFORMATION."—*The Scotsman.*

London: WARD, LOCK & CO., Salisbury Square, E.C.

HIGH CLASS BOOKS OF REFERENCE.

THE HAYDN SERIES OF MANUALS.

"THE MOST UNIVERSAL BOOK OF REFERENCE IN A MODERATE COMPASS THAT WE KNOW OF IN THE ENGLISH LANGUAGE."—*The Times.*

HAYDN'S DICTIONARY OF DATES. Relating to all Ages and Nations ; for Universal Reference. Containing about 10,000 distinct Articles, and 80,000 Dates and Facts. Sixteenth Edition, Enlarged. Corrected and Revised by BENJAMIN VINCENT, Librarian of the Royal Institution of Great Britain. In One thick Vol., medium 8vo, cloth, price 18s.; half-calf, 24s.; full or tree-calf, 31s. 6d.

"It is certainly no longer now a mere Dictionary of Dates, but A COMPREHENSIVE DICTIONARY OR ENCYCLOPÆDIA OF GENERAL INFORMATION."—*The Times.*

"It is BY FAR THE READIEST AND MOST RELIABLE WORK OF THE KIND."—*The Standard.*

VINCENT'S DICTIONARY OF BIOGRAPHY, Past and Present. Containing the Chief Events in the Lives of Eminent Persons of all Ages and Nations. By BENJAMIN VINCENT, Librarian of the Royal Institution of Great Britain, and Editor of "Haydn's Dictionary of Dates." In One thick Vol., medium 8vo, cloth, 7s. 6d.; half-calf, 12s.; full or tree-calf, 18s.

"It has the merit of condensing into the smallest possible compass the leading events in the career of every man and woman of eminence. . . . It is very carefully edited, and must evidently be the result of constant industry, combined with good judgment and taste."—*The Times.*

The CHEAPEST BOOK PUBLISHED *on* DOMESTIC MEDICINE, *&c.*
HAYDN'S DOMESTIC MEDICINE. By the late EDWIN LANKESTER, M.D., F.R.S., assisted by Distinguished Physicians and Surgeons. New Edition, including an Appendix on Sick Nursing and Mothers' Management. With 32 full pages of Engravings. In One Vol., medium 8vo, cloth gilt, 7s. 6d.; half-calf, 12s.

"Very exhaustive, and embodies an enormous amount of medical information in an intelligible shape."—*The Scotsman.*

"THE FULLEST AND MOST RELIABLE WORK OF ITS KIND."—*Liverpool Albion.*

HAYDN'S BIBLE DICTIONARY. For the use of all Readers and Students of the Old and New Testaments, and of the Apocrypha. Edited by the late Rev. CHARLES BOUTELL, M.A. New Edition, brought down to the latest date. With 100 pages of Engravings, separately printed on tinted paper. In One Vol., medium 8vo, cloth gilt, 7s. 6d.; half-calf, 12s.

"No better one than this is in the market. . . . Every local preacher should place this dictionary in his study, and every Sunday-school teacher should have it for reference."—*The Fountain.*

UNIFORM WITH "HAYDN'S BIBLE DICTIONARY."
WHISTON'S JOSEPHUS. An entirely New Library Edition of WILLIAM WHISTON'S translation of the Works of FLAVIUS JOSEPHUS. Comprising "The Antiquities of the Jews," and "The Wars of the Jews." With Memoir of the Author. Marginal Notes giving the Essence of the Narrative, and 100 pages of Engravings, separately printed on tinted paper. In One Vol., medium 8vo, cloth gilt, 7s. 6d.; half-calf, 12s.

"The present edition is cheap and good, being clearly printed, and, as already remarked, serviceably embellished with views and object drawings, not one of which is irrelevant to the matter."—*The Daily Telegraph.*

London: WARD, LOCK & CO., Salisbury Square, E.C.

THE PEOPLE'S STANDARD CYCLOPÆDIAS.

EVERYBODY'S LAWYER (Beeton's Law Book). Entirely New Edition, Revised by a BARRISTER. A Practical Compendium of the General Principles of English Jurisprudence; comprising upwards of 14,600 Statements of the Law. With a full Index, 27,000 References, every numbered paragraph in its particular place, and under its general head. Crown 8vo, 1,680 pp., cloth gilt, 7s. 6d.

⁎ *The sound practical information contained in this voluminous work is equal to that in a whole library of ordinary legal books, costing many guineas. Not only for every non-professional man in a difficulty are its contents valuable, but also for the ordinary reader, to whom a knowledge of the law is more important and interesting than is generally supposed.*

BEETON'S DICTIONARY OF GEOGRAPHY: A Universal Gazetteer. Illustrated by Maps – Ancient, Modern, and Biblical, and several Hundred Engravings in separate Plates on toned paper. Containing upwards of 12,000 distinct and complete Articles. Post 8vo, cloth gilt, 7s. 6d.; half-calf, 10s. 6d.

BEETON'S DICTIONARY OF BIOGRAPHY: Being the Lives of Eminent Persons of All Times. Containing upwards of 10,000 distinct and complete Articles, profusely Illustrated by Portraits. With the Pronunciation of Every Name. Post 8vo, cloth gilt, 7s. 6d.; half-calf, 10s. 6d.

BEETON'S DICTIONARY OF NATURAL HISTORY: A Popular and Scientific Account of Animated Creation. Containing upwards of 2,000 distinct and complete Articles, and more than 400 Engravings. With the Pronunciation of Every Name. Crown 8vo, cloth gilt, 7s. 6d.; half-calf, 10s. 6d.

BEETON'S BOOK OF HOME PETS: How to Rear and Manage in Sickness and in Health. With many Coloured Plates, and upwards of 200 Woodcuts from designs principally by HARRISON WEIR. With a Chapter on Ferns. Post 8vo, half-roan, 7s. 6d.; half-calf, 10s. 6d.

THE TREASURY OF SCIENCE, Natural and Physical. Comprising Natural Philosophy, Astronomy, Chemistry, Geology, Mineralogy, Botany, Zoology and Physiology. By F. SCHOEDLER, Ph.D. Translated and Edited by HENRY MEDLOCK, Ph.D., &c. With more than 500 Illustrations. Crown 8vo, cloth gilt, 7s. 6d.; half-calf, 10s. 6d.

A MILLION OF FACTS of Correct Data and Elementary Information concerning the entire Circle of the Sciences, and on all subjects of Speculation and Practice. By Sir RICHARD PHILLIPS. Carefully Revised and Improved. Crown 8vo, cloth gilt, 7s. 6d.; half-calf, 10s. 6d.

THE TEACHER'S PICTORIAL BIBLE AND BIBLE DICTIONARY. With the most approved Marginal References, and Explanatory Oriental and Scriptural Notes, Original Comments, and Selections from the most esteemed Writers. Illustrated with numerous Engravings and Coloured Maps. Crown 8vo, cloth gilt, red edges, 8s. 6d.; French morocco, 10s. 6d.; half-calf, 10s. 6d.; Turkey morocco, 15s.

THE SELF-AID CYCLOPÆDIA, for Self-Taught Students. Comprising General Drawing; Architectural, Mechanical, and Engineering Drawing; Ornamental Drawing and Design; Mechanics and Mechanism; the Steam Engine. By ROBERT SCOTT BURN, F.S.A.E., &c. With upwards of 1,000 Engravings. Demy 8vo, half-bound, price 10s. 6d.

London: WARD, LOCK & CO., Salisbury Square, E.C.

A NEW EDUCATIONAL WORK OF GREAT VALUE.

Just ready, folio, boards, price 5s., with 500 Original Wood Engravings.
WARD AND LOCK'S
PICTORIAL ATLAS OF NATURE.
MEN, ANIMALS, AND PLANTS OF ALL QUARTERS OF THE GLOBE.
For Home and School Use.

In no department of popular education has the progress that characterises our time been more distinctly marked than in the study of Geography; and nowhere have the enlarged views of the present day produced a more complete change in the method of tuition and in the scope of the subject. Geography must no longer be taught as a mere study of names, intermingled with certain statistical details of population, distances, measurements of altitudes, &c. A good geographical knowledge of any given quarter of the globe, or of a separate country, must now include a certain familiarity with the characteristic productions of the quarter or country in question, the types it presents in nations, animals, and plants. Thus, ETHNOGRAPHY, the study of races; ZOOLOGY, the study of animals; and BOTANY, the study of plants, are all to some extent associated with Geography.

In the improved state of the science of Geography, additional appliances have become necessary for its practical study. The atlas of maps, however complete it may be, only presents one aspect of the subject. The student now requires not only to understand the map that teaches him the topography of a country:— when he has made himself familiar with the surface of a part of the globe, *he requires to be taught what that region has to show as regards inhabitants and animal and vegetable productions.*

WARD AND LOCK'S PICTORIAL ATLAS OF NATURE has been prepared with a view of meeting this want. In a series of FIFTEEN LARGE PLATES it places before the eyes of the student the typical forms of the nations, animals, and plants of the various parts of the world. Each plate contains a map, around which the types are grouped; and numbers inserted in this map, and corresponding with others in the pictorial illustrations, show the learner where the races of men, and the plants and animals depicted, have their homes.

The greatest care has been taken to render the atlas strictly educational by the utmost accuracy and truth to nature in the pictures. *The plants have been drawn by botanical artists, the animals are not imaginative or fancy sketches, but zoologically correct, and the great majority of heads of men and women are from photographs taken from life, or else sketches from the note books of travellers, to whom the originals have sat.* In many cases the scale of proportion in which an animal or plant has been drawn is given. The animals are represented, where practicable, surrounded by the scenery of their native homes; besides the plants, the most important parts, such as flowers, fruit, leaves, &c., are separately given to draw the attention of the student especially to their curious or useful points.

Thus the ATLAS OF NATURE becomes a very necessary companion volume to the usual atlas of political geography.

In the schoolroom and the family circle alike it will be found most useful and welcome. A teacher, with one of these plates before him, has only to enlarge upon the notes which have been added in the form of suggestive information, to produce a lecture-lesson that can hardly fail to interest his class. Those engaged in tuition will readily see how much time and labour are saved, in the way of explanation, and how much more vivid an impression is produced than by words alone, when a picture of the object itself is placed before the learner, and his faculty of comparison and analysis is brought into action.

For self-tuition, those learners, now so numerous, who are educating themselves by means of manuals, will find WARD & LOCK'S ATLAS OF NATURE an ever present help, that will lighten their labours by conveying to the eye, in its clearly and correctly drawn pictures, the explanation of much they will find difficult in their books.

The utility of the ATLAS OF NATURE *is not confined to the study of geography even in its widest sense. The Student of Natural History, and of Botany, will find in it an equally useful and suggestive companion.*

London: WARD, LOCK & CO., Salisbury Square, E.C.

AN ENTIRELY NEW ETYMOLOGICAL DICTIONARY.

Just ready, demy 8vo, cloth, 5s.   WARD & LOCK'S

STANDARD

ETYMOLOGICAL DICTIONARY

OF THE ENGLISH LANGUAGE.

A POPULAR AND COMPREHENSIVE GUIDE TO THE PRONUNCIATION, PARTS OF SPEECH, MEANINGS, AND ETYMOLOGY OF ALL WORDS, ORDINARY, SCIENTIFIC, AND TECHNOLOGICAL NOW IN GENERAL USE.

With 40 pages of Engravings and an Appendix,

COMPRISING

1. ABBREVIATIONS USED IN WRITING AND PRINTING.
2. A BRIEF CLASSICAL DICTIONARY, COMPRISING THE PRINCIPAL DEITIES, HEROES, NOTABLE MEN AND WOMEN, &c., OF GREEK AND ROMAN MYTHOLOGY.
3. LETTERS: HOW TO BEGIN, END, AND ADDRESS THEM.
4. WORDS, PHRASES, AND PROVERBS, FROM THE LATIN, FREQUENTLY USED IN WRITING AND SPEAKING.
5. WORDS, PHRASES, AND PROVERBS, FROM THE FRENCH, WITH ENGLISH TRANSLATIONS.
6. WORDS, PHRASES, AND PROVERBS, FROM THE ITALIAN AND SPANISH WITH ENGLISH TRANSLATIONS.

Messrs. WARD, LOCK AND CO., in announcing this ENTIRELY NEW WORK, which has long been in preparation, desire to call special attention to the several points of excellence to be found in it, and feel sure that this valuable work will command the favour of the public. The following are the principal points to which attention is called :—

1. *Comprehensiveness.*—New words, that the progress of science, art, and philosophy has rendered necessary as additions to the vocabulary, and thousands of compound words have been introduced.

2. *Brevity.*—To ensure this, care has been taken to avoid redundancy of explanation, while every possible meaning of each word has been given.

3. *Pronunciation.*—Those who may use it will not be puzzled and confused with any arbitrary system of phonetic signs, similar to those usually found in Pronouncing Dictionaries. Every word of two syllables and more is properly divided and accented; and all *silent* letters are put in italics.

4. *Etymology.*—The words are arranged in groups, each group being placed under the principal word to which its members are closely allied. Words similarly spelt, but having distinct etymologies, are separated according to their derivation.

5. *Illustrations.*—40 pages of Illustrations of various objects given, to assist students in arriving at a clear perception of that which is indicated by the name.

London: *WARD, LOCK & CO.*, Salisbury Square, **E.C.**

WARD & LOCK'S POPULAR DICTIONARIES.

THE STANDARD DICTIONARIES OF LANGUAGE.

WEBSTER'S UNIVERSAL PRONOUNCING AND DEFINING DICTIONARY OF THE ENGLISH LANGUAGE. Condensed from Noah Webster's Large Work, with numerous Synonyms, carefully discriminated by CHAUNCEY A. GOODRICH, D.D. With Walker's Key to the Pronunciation of Classical and Scriptural Proper Names; a Vocabulary of Modern Geographical Names; Phrases and Quotations from the Ancient and Modern Languages; Abbreviations, &c. Royal 8vo, half bound, 5s.; demy 8vo, cloth, 3s. 6d.

"This Dictionary must commend itself to every intelligent reader. . . . . Let us add, it is carefully and well printed, and very cheap; and having said so much, we feel assured that further recommendation is unnecessary. It is good, useful, and cheap."—*Liverpool Mail.*

WEBSTER'S IMPROVED PRONOUNCING DICTIONARY OF THE ENGLISH LANGUAGE. Condensed and adapted to English Orthography and Usage, with additions by CHARLES ROBSON. To which are added, Accentuated Lists of Scriptural, Classical, and Modern Geographical Proper Names. Cloth, price 2s. 6d.; strongly half-bound, 3s. 6d.

WEBSTER'S POCKET PRONOUNCING DICTIONARY OF THE ENGLISH LANGUAGE. Condensed from the Original Dictionary by NOAH WEBSTER, LL.D.; with Accentuated Vocabularies of Classical, Scriptural, and Modern Geographical Names. Revised Edition, by WILLIAM G. WEBSTER, Son of Noah Webster. Containing 10,000 more words than "Walker's Dictionary." Royal 16mo, cloth, price 1s.

WARD & LOCK'S POCKET SHILLING DICTIONARY OF THE ENGLISH LANGUAGE. Condensed by CHARLES ROBSON, from NOAH WEBSTER's Original Work. With Accentuated Lists of Scripture and Modern Geographical Proper Names. Super-royal 32mo, cloth, 768 pp., 1s.

WARD AND LOCK'S SHILLING DICTIONARY OF THE GERMAN LANGUAGE. Containing German-English and English-German, Geographical Dictionary, Table of Coins, &c. Super-royal 32mo, cloth, 900 pp., 1s.

WEBSTER'S SIXPENNY POCKET PRONOUNCING DICTIONARY OF THE ENGLISH LANGUAGE. Condensed from the Original Dictionary by NOAH WEBSTER, LL.D.; with Accentuated Vocabularies of Classical, Scriptural, and Modern Geographical Names. Revised Edition, by WILLIAM G. WEBSTER, Son of Noah Webster. Strongly bound in cloth, price 6d.

WEBSTER'S PENNY PRONOUNCING DICTIONARY OF THE ENGLISH LANGUAGE. Exhibiting the Spelling, Pronunciation, Part of Speech, and Meaning of all Words in General Use among English-speaking Nations. Containing over 10,000 words. Price 1d.; or, linen wrapper, 2d.

London: WARD, LOCK & CO., Salisbury Square, E.C.

ETIQUETTE BOOKS.

THE STANDARD ETIQUETTE BOOKS.

THE MANNERS OF POLITE SOCIETY; or, Etiquette for Ladies, Gentlemen, and Families. A Complete Guide to Visiting, Entertaining, and Travelling, Conversation, the Toilette, Courtship, &c.; with Hints on Marriage, Music, Domestic Affairs, &c. Crown 8vo, elegantly bound, cloth gilt, 3s. 6d.

ALL ABOUT ETIQUETTE; or, The Manners of Polite Society: for Ladies, Gentlemen, and Families; Courtship, Correspondence, Carving, Dining, Dress, Ball Room, Marriage, Parties, Riding, Travelling, Visiting, &c. &c. Crown 8vo, cloth gilt, 2s. 6d.

THE COMPLETE ETIQUETTE FOR LADIES. A Guide to Visiting, Entertaining, and Travelling: with Hints on Courtship, Marriage, and Dress; In the Street, Shopping, At Church, Visiting, Conversation, Obligations to Gentlemen, Presents, Dinners, Travelling, Offers and Refusals, Correspondence, Courtship, Marriage, &c. Post 8vo, cloth, 1s.

THE COMPLETE ETIQUETTE FOR GENTLEMEN. A Guide to the Table, the Toilette, and the Ball Room; with Hints on Courtship, Music, and Manners, In the Street, Attendance on Ladies, Visiting, Dress, Dinners, Carving, Wines, the Ball Room, Buying and Selling, the Smoking and Billiard Rooms, &c. Post 8vo, cloth, 1s.

THE COMPLETE ETIQUETTE FOR FAMILIES. A Guide to Conversation, Parties, Travel, and the Toilette; with Hints on Domestic Affairs. Post 8vo, cloth, 1s.

HOSTESS AND GUEST. A Guide to the Etiquette of Dinners, Suppers, Luncheons, the Precedence of Guests, &c. With numerous Engravings. Fcap. 8vo, ornamental wrapper, 1s.; cloth gilt, 1s. 6d.

THE "HOW" HANDBOOKS.

Elegantly bound in cloth, gilt edges, with beautifully Coloured Frontispiece, price 6d. each; or in wrapper, 3d.

1. How to Dance; or, Etiquette of the Ball Room.
2. How to Woo; or, The Etiquette of Courtship and Marriage.
3. How to Dress; or, The Etiquette of the Toilet.
4. How to Dine; or, Etiquette of the Dinner Table.
5. How to Manage; or, Etiquette of the Household.
6. How to Entertain; or, Etiquette for Visitors.
7. How to Behave; or, The Etiquette of Society.
8. How to Travel; or, Etiquette for Ship, Rail, Coach, or Saddle.

*** *These elegant and attractive little Manuals will be found useful Text-Books for the subjects to which they refer; they are full of suggestive hints, and are undoubtedly superior to any hitherto published.*

London: *WARD, LOCK & CO., Salisbury Square, E.C.*

ILLUSTRATED POETICAL WORKS.

"The power of English Literature is in its Poets."

MOXON'S POPULAR POETS.

NEW AND ENLARGED EDITIONS, with Red Border Lines, Critical Memoirs by WILLIAM MICHAEL ROSSETTI, and Illustrations.

The press and the public, alike in Great Britain and her Colonies, and in the United States, unite in their testimony to the immense superiority of Messrs. Moxon's Popular Poets over any other similar collections published by any other house. Their possession of the Copyright works of Coleridge, Hood, Keats, Shelley, Wordsworth, and other great National Poets, places this series above rivalry.

1. Byron's Poetical Works.
2. Longfellow's Poetical Works.
3. Wordsworth's Poetical Works.
4. Scott's Poetical Works.
5. Shelley's Poetical Works.
6. Moore's Poetical Works.
7. Hood's Poetical Works.
8. Keats' Poetical Works.
9. Coleridge's Poetical Works.
10. Burns' Poetical Works.
11. Tupper's Proverbial Philosophy. The Four Series Complete in One Vol., with Portrait.
12. Milton's Poetical Works.
13. Campbell's Poetical Works.
14. Pope's Poetical Works.
15. Cowper's Poetical Works.
16. Humorous Poems.
17. American Poems.
18. Mrs. Hemans' Poetical Works.
19. Thomson's Poetical Works.
20. Poetic Treasures.
21. Hood's Poetical Works. Second Series.
22. J. G. Whittier's Poetical Works.
23. J. R. Lowell's Poetical Works.
24. Young's Poetical Works.
25. Shakespeare's Complete Works.
26. Keble's Christian Year.
27. Poe's Poetical Works.

With Red Border Lines, Critical Memoir, and Illustrations, handsomely bound, cloth gilt, gilt edges,

PRICE 3s. 6d. PER VOLUME.

Also to be had in the following varieties of binding—Morocco, 7s. 6d.; morocco extra, 8s.; tree calf, 10s. 6d.; relief leather, 12s.

MOXON'S FIVE SHILLING POETS.

Crown 8vo, cloth gilt, bevelled boards, gilt top, 5s.; half-morocco, 6s.

Hood's Serious Poems. With Preface by THOMAS HOOD the Younger, and numerous Illustrations.

Hood's Comic Poems. With Preface by THOMAS HOOD the Younger, and numerous Illustrations.

Shelley's Poetical Works. With Portrait.

Keats' Poetical Works. With a Memoir by Lord HOUGHTON.

Longfellow's Poetical Works. With Memoir by WILLIAM MICHAEL ROSSETTI. Illustrated.

Scott's Poetical Works. With Memoir by WILLIAM MICHAEL ROSSETTI. Illustrated.

Hood's Poetical Works. 1st Series. With Memoir by WILLIAM MICHAEL ROSSETTI. Illustrated.

London: WARD, LOCK & CO., Salisbury Square, E.C.

www.ingramcontent.com/pod-product-compliance
Lightning Source LLC
Chambersburg PA
CBHW021355230426
43666CB00006B/529